baptism
by toilet water

baptism by toilet water

JAMES F. WINTER

TATE PUBLISHING & *Enterprises*

Published by Tate Publishing & Enterprises, LLC
127 E. Trade Center Terrace | Mustang, Oklahoma 73064 USA
1.888.361.9473 | www.tatepublishing.com

Tate Publishing is committed to excellence in the publishing industry. The company reflects the philosophy established by the founders, based on Psalm 68:11,
"The Lord gave the word and great was the company of those who published it."

Book design copyright © 2010 by Tate Publishing, LLC. All rights reserved.
Cover design by Chris Webb
Interior design by Jeff Fisher

Published in the United States of America

ISBN: 978-1-61663-980-8
1. Biography & Autobiography, Personal Memoirs
2. Family & Relationships, Abuse, General
10.09.16

Dedication

This book is dedicated to my children, Tyler, Mallory, and Zachary Winter. My hope is that within these pages they will find and embrace the legacy of the family they never knew.

I would also like to extend a special thanks to my wife, Aimee, for without her steadfast love and support, the completion of this book would not have been possible.

Acknowledgments

First and foremost I wish to thank God for his unconditional love for me. I would also like to thank Diane Flack, whose contributions, direction, and advice were vital to the completion of this project. To Mary Ann Bowles, for her relentless editing assistance, which ultimately transformed my book into a polished product. To my sister, Kerry Sedivy, for her support and for being there when I could not. To my uncle, John Winter, first for his encouragement, and secondly for being my personal historian. John provided a treasure trove of historical family documents, which proved invaluable to the accuracy of this work. To my uncle, Jim Winter, for shedding light on several pivotal stories in the book. To Jim Cottral, for being the best friend a guy could ever have. Had it not been for Jim, the completion of my story would not have been possible. And last but certainly not least, to James Miller, for his mentoring and being my strongest supporter, especially during the infancy of my book.

If the Lord delights in a man's way, he makes his steps firm; though he stumble, he will not fall, for the Lord upholds him with his hand.

Psalm 37:23–24 (NIV)

Table of Contents

Preface

Experiencing the loss of a loved one is an undeniably life-changing event that challenges a person's capacity to endure emotional pain. It's only a matter of time before each one of us will have to travel down this road, which eventually ends with the permanent separation from someone for whom we've deeply cared. Our first encounter with death often comes during childhood, usually in the form of a grandparent or an elderly neighbor whose time has come to an end. We begin to form an understanding of what death is and how it reveals the fragility of our own mortality. We are unable to ignore its implications of finality and are soon forced to come to grips with how it can render us powerless when we are in its presence.

Death, like water, can take many forms. Death can be slow and drawn out or it could happen in the time it takes to blow out a candle. It can be agonizing or relatively painless; at least, this is what we are led to believe. In either case, the end result is that for the rest of our natural-born lives we will become separated from someone for whom we knew and cared. For those who survive, it's a sudden realization that a door in their life has been slammed shut, never to be opened again for as long as we live. Immediately, feelings of sadness, loneliness, despair, and heartache envelop us. These feelings can intensify, especially when the loss is someone close, such as a parent, spouse, sibling, or child. These powerful feelings are often accompanied with regrets. The worst of these is guilt. We can become branded by guilt for not giving them more of our time while they were still in the world. Such an experience can leave a person devastated. Imagine, if you can, having to go through this tragic process in repetitive fashion. I did just that as, one by one, my family perished around me.

Within these pages you will learn how I was broken and then miraculously reconstructed by what I like to refer to as "heavenly forces outside of my own control." This book serves as a testimony to the lives of my family and the struggles I shared with them before, during, and after their deaths. It's extremely important their story is told, for even in death they have much to offer. I will attempt with the best of my ability to share with you the incredible example of their extraordinary bravery that they dauntlessly exhibited during their lives and in the face of death. I suffered through the loss of seven family members, an experience only overshadowed by an extremely difficult period in which five of them died in a seven-year span.

Before delving into the story, it's important to acknowledge the central theme that continually reappears throughout this book. This recurring theme is how good can come from bad. On the surface, most people view this statement as an oxymoron since it clearly represents a stark contradiction. However, if you look deeper, you'll often find some measure of good directly resulting from something bad that's taken place. It's what I have come to believe is a preset counterbalance or a slingshot effect that prevents our world from swaying too far in either direction. Keep in mind there are exceptions to every rule and clearly there is no scientific proof to substantiate such a theory. However, I will say in my own personal experience, I have found it to be remarkably accurate.

History provides many examples that help support my theory of good coming from bad. The most defining of these would be the sorrowful death Jesus Christ endured when he gave his life on the cross. For Christians, although his death was tragic, his personal sacrifice atoned for the sins of the world and forever opened the doors of heaven to all. Could there ever be a more profound example of good coming from bad? If you're not a Christian, it's still hard to deny how his words, deeds, and death have inspired the world for two millennia. The Bible is filled with many such examples of this theory, but we can also look at recent history right here in the United States that further substantiates my claim.

The American Civil War was without question the bloodiest conflict the United States has ever endured. More Americans died in the Civil War than all other wars combined. The war symbolized everything evil man is capable of; yet, when we look at what resulted from it, we find great achievements such as the abolishment of slavery and the reunification of a divided nation. Abraham Lincoln is revered by many as the greatest president who ever lived. His achievements as a president could not have been possible without the war. In fact, there may have never been a Gettysburg Address or an Emancipation Proclamation had these events not taken place.

I would be remiss not to provide an application of this theory to modern times. The recent events of September 11, 2001, remain vivid in the minds of all Americans. These events also serve as a fresh example of how good can come from bad. For those Americans who gave their lives on that frightful day, our country will forever be in debt to their sacrifice. Let's not forget how further destruction was averted by the heroic deeds of the passengers of United Airlines Flight 93. They did not die in vain. Their sacrifice showed the world that freedom couldn't be suppressed. Through their terrible loss, patriotism soared, reuniting a grieving nation. Human history is filled with many such examples. I challenge you to look there and in your own personal life history. If you're honest with yourself, you'll find when this theory is put to the test, it almost always contains some measure of truth. The pages that follow reveal how this ongoing process impacted my life and how I eventually came to understand that not everything is lost with death.

I have a multitude of memories of my loved ones who have since passed on from this world. Many are fond; some are not. Through it all, I became a witness to their lives. Over time, I realized these experiences carried with them the responsibility of keeping their story alive. As stated in the dedication that precedes this preface, I wrote this book first and foremost for my children. My secondary purpose was to share my experience with those who have yet to attain closure, hoping it may offer solace to them. Lastly, I offer it to those who have yet to face death, so they are not completely ill-prepared when they are confronted by it.

This book is an odyssey of life and death. I have painstakingly cross-referenced my recollections with those of surviving relatives to ensure the most accurate portrayal possible. Anything less would be a shameful disservice to what their lives have come to stand for. With utmost sincerity, it is now my privilege to tell you our story.

No Turning Back

Grueling doubts soaked my conscience during the hot summer months of 1988. I had just made a monumental decision to move my family from Iowa to Florida, where the prospect of good-paying jobs in a tropical paradise awaited us. Up to that point, it was the biggest decision I had made in my life and with it came a flood of apprehensions. Would we be able to survive and make a go of it? What unknown challenges awaited us? How would my children handle the change? Deep down inside, I was convinced this was our best way out of a substandard life.

Beyond the normal worries of such an endeavor came the saddening reality that I was leaving behind my immediate family and friends. This included my parents, sisters, good friends, but most of all, my brother John, who I had become especially close to over the years. At the time, he had just turned thirty-two and I was twenty-eight. Because of our closeness, neither one of us spoke much of my impending departure. When it was time to leave, instead of being glum he focused on our reunion. He had already made plans to visit sometime in the fall. I looked forward to that day.

What followed was something neither of us could have ever imagined. Just over a month after leaving, he was diagnosed with a rare strain of lymphatic cancer. Upon hearing the news, I couldn't help feel that I had just made the worst mistake of my life by moving to Florida. Reversing my course was not an option. We had invested everything in the move. There was no turning back now. Financially strapped, I did the only thing I could. I started scrounging for any money I could find to put toward a plane ticket to get back home. It was my only option.

Since our contact was limited to phone conversations, we called each other often. Being restricted to audio updates drove me crazy, for I was unable to see the physical changes he was undergoing. It would take nine long months before I could come up with the money for a roundtrip ticket to Iowa and back. When I finally did, things were actually looking up. My brother's leukemia had been in remission for a few months. He was even allowed to return home, providing he took it easy. In addition to this good news was the prospect of a bone marrow transplant. Bone marrow transplants were a relatively new procedure at the time, but had already yielded some promising results. When I returned home, my sisters and I would undergo testing to determine if any of us could serve as a compatible donor.

I flew into Dubuque during the late spring of 1989. The season of spring brought with it the quality of renewal, instilling new hope that John could win his struggle with cancer. After my flight landed I was overjoyed to see him waiting for me at the airport. It was obvious he had lost some weight, but considering what he had been through, he looked pretty good. Seeing him rebounding from his initial setback eased my worries a bit. We spent the majority of our time catching up on the previous nine months we'd been apart. Our reunion lifted our spirits, but it was cut short by the testing. I could hardly complain, though; the lost time was well worth the chance of my prayers being answered. My sisters and I were tested in the afternoon on the day of my departure. This meant I would have to wait for the test results until after I returned to Florida. I embraced him as we said our goodbyes. I was still very worried for him, but I believed I was leaving on a high note. With four siblings being tested, I felt the odds were good that one of us would be a compatible donor for the bone marrow transplant.

Upon returning, it didn't take long for me to hear the results. My mother called a day or two later. I could tell by the tone in her voice that the news was not good. I was devastated when she told me that none of us qualified as a suitable donor. Worse yet, within weeks of my return, his cancer had returned full blown.

When I spoke to John on the phone, I was unable to conceal my concern over the recent turn of events. He told me not to worry. Instead, he told me to have faith in his ability to overcome his cancer. He spoke with a determined resolve in his voice. I reasoned if he could stay positive, then I surely had to as well.

Another eight months went by without laying eyes on my brother. It was now mid-January of 1990. I couldn't help but see the irony in the contrasting environments in which we lived. Here I was in sunny Florida surrounded by tall palm trees and sandy beaches. He, on the other hand, was confined to a hospital room with only one window whose view consisted of frozen tundra and barren cornfields. Each of our environments reflected our state of health. It was like a bad premonition. Everyone around me who knew of his situation kept warning me his chances for survival were slim. I refused to give up hope. I knew he was a fighter. If anyone could overcome cancer, it was certainly him.

For so long now our contact had been limited to scheduled phone conversations. Our physical separation clouded my perceptions of what was happening. Unable to see his deterioration, the reality of the situation remained hidden from me. Furthermore, during our many hours of phone conversations, he performed like a top-notch surgeon to skillfully remove even the most residual of doubts that I harbored over his recovery. His will to live convinced me he could and would beat his cancer. I, like the fool, fell for it hook, line, and sinker. Looking back on it, his motives became crystal clear. He was doing everything in his power to make things easier on me. He was more than willing to pay the price of carrying his burden alone if it meant sparing me from enduring any suffering over what was happening to him.

John wasn't entirely alone. However, like me, he was distanced from everyone who was close to him, just not as far. The hospital at which he was staying was in Iowa City, Iowa. This was the closest major hospital in the region equipped with cancer treatment facilities. It was located two and a half hours from the rest of the immediate family. His fiancée, Maria, lived in Dubuque, which was a little less than two hours away. John had been with Maria for a number of years. She was a beautiful Italian girl with whom he had fallen in love several years before his cancer had taken hold of him. Maria did make visits, but it was extremely difficult for her to watch John slowly wither away. Her father had recently died of cancer and the wounds from that experience were still very fresh.

During these months apart from him I had been saving again, preparing for another visit sometime in late April. However, at the beginning of that month, I received an urgent call from him insisting I come now. I had the money for the flight but not enough for any other expenditure, such as a hotel room. He told me not to worry about the hotel. He had already made arrangements for me to stay at the hospital. I wasn't overly thrilled at the prospect of being put up in the hospital, but the tone in his voice was a clear signal that he wanted me to come now. I had to inform my boss of the change in plans, but he was fully aware of the situation, so it posed no problems. I would soon be on my way back to Iowa.

For the first time in quite a while I felt those familiar uneasy feelings return. I tried to brush them off but I couldn't. I sensed nothing but dread. Before hanging up he made a final request. He begged me to bring my five-year-old son Tyler with me. Prior to our departure from Dubuque, John had developed a strong bond with Tyler. Not wanting to disappoint him, I told him I'd do my best, knowing full well there was zero chance of Tyler coming along. I simply couldn't afford another plane ticket.

✝

When Tyler was born, John took an immediate interest in the boy. I'm certain his interest to be connected to a child was partly brought about from his recent divorce. John had met and married his wife, Debbie, while they were stationed together in the army. Their union produced a daughter, Sarah, who with her mother, moved to California shortly after the divorce. If I close my eyes I can still see the pain on his face the day they left Dubuque for California. Their absence left a huge void in his life, but he was able to fill part of that void through my son.

Although the absence of Sarah was the major reason for his heavy heart, there was definitely a unique connection between him and Tyler. Shortly after Tyler was born, John started showing up at my place a lot more. When Tyler reached the toddler stage, it wasn't uncommon for him to take my son for a weekend. On one such occasion, I can recall him picking up Tyler on a Friday and then vanishing without a trace until late Sunday evening. John was definitely not a stay-at-home kind of a guy. In those days cell phones didn't exist, but this was hardly an excuse for not checking in with us. I can remember being infuriated with him for not contacting us over the entire weekend. Once I got past his blatant irresponsibility, I actually found this episode amusing. Deep down inside I could never stay mad at him for very long anyway. Seeing him take an active role in Tyler's life meant the world to both Tyler and me. Tyler had become equally fond of John as well. I loved to watch their unbridled play each time the two of them got together. Their favorite pastime was wrestling. John would customarily put up a terrific fight before succumbing to a barrage of blows from Tyler. This scene was played out countless times, but they never seemed to tire of it.

✝

A few weeks before my trip to Iowa, Sarah had flown in with Debbie from California to visit John. That visit meant the world to him. He had missed his daughter terribly, but seeing her made him realize how blessed he was to be the father of such a beautiful girl. His heart would get heavy whenever he spoke of her. Being a father myself, I could totally relate. I felt so bad for him. I couldn't imagine being separated from my children.

The next day I kissed my family goodbye. I boarded the plane at Miami International Airport and began my journey to the hospital at the University of Iowa, in Iowa City. When I found my seat, an ominous feeling came over me. Feeling weak, I reached for the one comfort I had, my Bible. I tightly gripped the leather-bound book and began searching its pages for strength in my time of need. I felt shallow, for seldom did I seek it when things were going well.

My thoughts were soon drowned out by the thundering engines from other planes preparing to take off into the wild blue yonder. In turn, my jet began its stroll down the runway, jockeying itself for takeoff. A few moments later, I heard the engines begin to rev. Simultaneously I closed my Bible and my eyes as the jet built up speed for liftoff. When it comes to flying, takeoffs and landings have always been nervous moments for me. During the ascent as the plane reached the clouds, I couldn't resist the thought that I was moving closer to God. Once my plane reached its set altitude, I felt a little more at ease. I thought to myself, *Pray now*, for there would never be a better chance for God to hear me. As I flew through the clouds I pleaded, bargained, and even begged for God to save him.

For quite some time I remained fixated on John until I heard the scratchy sound of the pilot's voice coming over the intercom, informing the passengers that we had just crossed Tennessee. I had hoped we were further. Peering out the window, I laid down my Bible to see a startling sight. Lush, green fields with swiftly moving rivers suddenly gave way to ice, snow, and the dead of winter. All life was virtually swallowed up by the encroaching lifeless landscape. These stark changes in scenery prompted a feeling of foreboding. It felt like I had entered a dead zone. The dark feeling I encountered earlier in the flight returned. I struggled to ward off these invasive thoughts. I found myself reaching for the security of my Bible again. Randomly opening it, there, right before my very eyes, was the help I so desperately needed. It was the last verse of the last page in the book of Matthew. It was Jesus, saying, "I am with you always, even to the end of the age."

My plane finally touched down at the tiny airport in Iowa City. I quickly gathered my luggage and boarded the shuttle bus that took me to the hospital. My mind was racing with thoughts, which included how relieved I was that the flight was finally over. More important was the anticipation of our long-awaited reunion. It had been almost a year since I last laid eyes on him. I hurriedly made my way through the hospital entrance to locate the information desk so I could find his room. After a short time, I was summoned by an attractive young, female receptionist. She put my anxieties to rest by offering to take me to my brother's room. Pungent medicinal smells filled the air as we made our way through a series of twisting and turning hallways that resembled catacombs. When we finally arrived at his room, I was met by an intern who confirmed I was in the right place. The moment had come. I was finally going to see him.

I slowly opened the door and in a quiet voice I called out for him, but there was no reply. As I crossed the threshold of his door, nothing could have prepared me for the sight I was now seeing. The once dynamic, good-looking, muscular, dark-haired, two-hundred-plus-pound man I had come to love and admire as my brother was almost unrecognizable. His head was nearly bald except for a few straggling hairs that pointed in opposite directions. His eyes were sunken to the bone, the color of his skin was a faded yellow, and he looked like he was eighty years old. I stared at him in complete disbelief. The utter shock of what I was now seeing grabbed a hold of me, refusing to let go. My eyes quickly scanned the entire length of his body. I could see several places where his robe failed to cover his body, exposing his emaciated frame. My worst fears materialized as I came to grips with the truth I had denied myself for so long. He was dying. Speechless, the irreversible reality of the situation began to overwhelm me. I felt paralyzed. How could I have been so naive? How could I have ever allowed myself to believe everything was just going to be fine?

As I sat by his bedside, I wanted so badly to wake him. Mortified by his appearance, I remained silent. Shaking my head in disbelief, I now struggled mightily with the false sense of security I had held on to for so long. How could I have let myself believe that he would easily defeat this terrible thing? I was now being bombarded by unrelenting waves of guilt crashing through to the core of my very being. The realization of him enduring most of this hardship on his own was more than I could handle. It was the absolute low point in my life.

While I sat there wallowing in my shame, his eyes slowly opened. A half smile came over his face. I reached for his hand as I fought off my tears. We looked each other in the eye, and the first words he spoke to me were, "Did you bring the boy?" I felt like I had just been punched in the gut. I had now surpassed what I had just thought was the lowest point in my life. I squeaked out a weak apology, telling him it just wasn't possible. I tried to be strong, but I could feel the wetness begin to drench my face. I did not cry openly, but the tears were streaming down my face. The pain I was feeling could not have been more obvious to him. Just like the big brother he had always been, he looked up at me and said, "It's okay. You're here."

During the rest of my stay I never mentioned the topic of my son again. It hurt too much to face up to the fact I had denied him the one thing he had ever asked from me during his entire struggle. I did my best to change the subject by forcing out the words, "It's good to see you." He repeated my words almost in unison. This was followed up with a lengthy embrace. I wept openly at this point. He told me, "It's okay. We're together now." I didn't want to let go of him, but somehow I collected myself and remembered that it was I who was supposed to be comforting him. The irony of this was almost too much. When I slowly released him from my grip, I noticed him wincing in pain. It was obvious that even the slightest touch brought him discomfort. I knew from here on in as difficult as it was, I had to restrain myself from touching him.

The next couple of days were very difficult for me. It seemed at every turn I was denied of even the least bit of quality time with him. He was undergoing so many tests that I had to settle for a few fragmented moments that were continually interrupted by hospital personnel coming and going. I distinctly recall one day where I made more than half a dozen unsuccessful trips back and forth, hoping to steal a little time with him. Each time I was met by either a nurse or technician who informed me he was undergoing tests and to try back in an hour or so. I knew it wasn't their fault, but I became increasingly agitated with the reality that our time together was slowly ticking away.

The room I stayed in was located in a subterranean level of the hospital. To get there I had to descend a flight of stairs. It made me think of an old black and white movie I had seen as a kid where a similar descent led to an abysmal dungeon. The room was equally depressing. It wasn't much bigger than a child's room. The walls however were unusually high, so much so it made the room appear strangely disproportionate. The walls were empty and painted an ugly, drab, green color. Adding to this was the frigid temperature of the room that was illuminated by a single low-watt light bulb. Whenever I was away from him I spent most of my time reading my Bible, searching the Scriptures for inner strength and guidance. When reading in the room, I would lie in the metal-framed bed that had been furnished for me. The silence was deafening. Had it not been for the creaking noise the bed made each time I repositioned myself, there would have been no sound at all. I tried to block out my surroundings, but to no avail. After a time, I decided to flee my sunken chamber and do my soul searching somewhere else.

I made my way through the endless corridors in search of a less dismal place. My quest came to an abrupt end when the same young lady who had escorted me to my brother's room the first day I arrived called out to me again, saying, "Mr. Winter, your brother is looking for you. He's back in his room now if you would like to see him." I thanked her and then wasted no time in getting back to his room.

While making my way to his room, I tried to come up with a few things to talk about. It ended up being of little consequence; he was so exhausted from his testing he had no energy for conversation. Upset by what he was being put through, I asked him, "What purpose does it possibly serve to endure all of this poking and prodding?" He told me he had offered himself to his doctors as a human guinea pig so they could conduct whatever experiments they desired, in the hopes it might help someone else in the future. He had arranged, with the permission of his doctors, to have the bulk of this testing done earlier in the week so we could have my last couple of days together. Once again I was humbled by my own selfishness. I stayed with him for the remainder of the day. For the most part, I kept silent so he could rest.

The next two days were filled with priceless conversation. While I sat and listened to him speak of days gone by, I treasured each precious word that rolled off his lips. Precious words indeed. I still thank God for giving me these moments with him. We continued to sit for hours reminiscing over glory days. The fondest of these memories was the month-long vacation we took together when we were in our twenties.

✝

The year was 1982. We were living together as roommates in Dubuque, Iowa. Earlier that year I had been working in central Illinois for a grocery store chain when I was let go for coming in late. I called him shortly after I was fired. He couldn't have been happier with the news. He told me it was time for me to come home, and I was welcome to stay with him for as long as it took me to get back on my feet. My damaged ego kept me from calling it quits right away. My first instinct was to stick it out awhile. I thought maybe I'd get lucky and find a new job. When the job market proved bleak, I succumbed to his invitation. I have to admit the prospect of being his roommate softened my pride. Although I would remain virtually unemployed for at least a year, the time we shared together proved more valuable than any job offer.

Shortly after I moved in, he hatched a plan for us to take a trip out west in the spring of 1983. For two years he had saved all of his vacation time. It amounted to a little more than a month. Since I was unemployed, time off was the one thing I had in plentiful supply.

The vacation occurred at a pivotal time for both of us. I was unemployed and practically penniless, searching for a way out of my futility. He, on the other hand, had a very comfortable life making a good wage as a physician's assistant. However, he was clearly discontented with the path he was on. As crazy as it sounds, he was more than eager to trade in his medical career for a chance to pursue his dream of becoming a stand-up comedian.

Neither of us would require any coaxing to make this trip. Just the thought of spending a month together on a long adventure was more than enough incentive. For him, the trip was two-fold; he desperately wanted to see his daughter Sarah in California, but he also wanted to take a stab at his dream of performing as a stand-up comedian. He truly felt this was his calling. He believed by performing at the popular comedy clubs of Los Angeles, he would have a reliable measuring stick to determine if he had the right stuff.

For me the trip offered a golden opportunity to not only explore but photograph the national parks of the west. I had always been a nature freak. My love for photography was the only thing that exceeded this passion. Over the past couple of years I had acquired the camera and the lenses that would make this trip unforgettable for me.

Everything was a go. Our starting date was April 1 and our return date was April 30. We embarked on our adventure right on schedule. We would make the roughly 4,000-mile trek in my brother's black 1976 Ford pick-up truck. He had recently installed a white cab cover to hold our belongings. "The truck," as my brother's vehicle became affectionately known, seemed to be blessed with uncanny luck. In time, I came to realize luck had little to do with it.

The first incident of "the truck's" good fortune manifested itself in the mountains of Colorado. We had stopped in Denver to visit a few of John's old army buddies. After our visit, we departed from Denver just before sunset. We were following Interstate 70 just past Grand Junction when a light snow began to fall. An hour later, the light snow had turned into a blizzard. The farther we traveled, the heavier it fell. Before long our visibility was reduced to a few feet. Now if you've ever been caught driving in a blizzard, you know how scary that can be. But if you're driving in a blizzard in the mountains, that's downright terrifying! We were now moving at a snail's pace; it was pitch black, and the road was only discernable by the dissipating tire tracks left behind by the vehicles that had preceded us.

Nervously, we weighed our options. There weren't many. Then, suddenly in the distance, we saw a bright light like a beacon. As we approached it, we could make out the outline of a huge building. It was a summer resort that was closed for the winter. I couldn't help but make comparisons to the movie *The Shining.* We pulled off anyway and hunkered down for the night in the back of his truck. John had thrown a bunch of old sleeping bags in the back of the cab before leaving Iowa. What a sight they were now. It was cold, but we survived the night and awoke the next day to sunny skies and a cleanly plowed Interstate 70.

Further on in our trek toward California, we were traveling through a desolate area in Nevada when "the truck" began to overheat. We were extremely worried, for the next oasis was over forty miles away. We shut the air conditioner off in an attempt to lessen the duress on the overheated engine. However, it only served to prolong the inevitable as we continued to watch the temperature gauge creep closer and closer to the red danger zone. We looked each other in the eye, silently acknowledging it was only a matter of time before we'd be stranded. But then, right as we had lost hope, several menacing clouds appeared out of nowhere. Within seconds a heavy rain started coming down. This mysterious rain cooled off the engine, causing the needle on the gauge to plunge. Astounded by the miraculous turn of events, I no longer believed in dumb luck. This was nothing short of divine intervention. Someone was definitely looking out for us. This trip confirmed that God was alive and well. We cruised into the next oasis and gave the radiator a well-deserved drink. We returned to the road with no further incidents. .

Perhaps the greatest example of our godly administering didn't come until the very end of our 4,000-mile trek. We had pulled over to fill the gas tank one last time before arriving in Dubuque.

While at the station, I noticed a rock that was lodged in one of John's tires. As I was removing it, to my complete surprise, I didn't see a spare tire underneath the cab. Perplexed, I asked him where his spare was located. He told me he had intended on getting one before we left, but it had completely slipped his mind. In utter disbelief I said, "You mean we crossed endless mountain ranges, deserts, and gorges without a spare tire?" With a smirk he replied, "Just goes to show that what you don't know can't hurt you."

The trip proved to be more than just an exercise in survival. It opened our eyes to the vast natural beauty of our country. For me, exploring the west was a dream come true, where each horizon offered a different reward. The feeling I experienced as I encountered the endless treasure trove of parks and natural areas could only be described as euphoric. Playing the role of the never satisfied adventurer, I kept suggesting side trips off the beaten path. At first John was hesitant to go along with my unplanned excursions, but he eventually gave in because he knew it was important to me. He seemed more focused on getting to our destination rather than exploring. However, once he began tasting the fruits of the west, he became putty in my hands. I furthered his interest by letting him take some photos with my camera. The wide-angle lens I purchased the year before profoundly complimented the incomparable scenery. It instantly brought his appreciation to new heights. I knew he was completely absorbed when he said, "I had no idea how powerful the effect of nature had on the soul. You have given me a view into a world I never knew existed." I could not have received a better compliment. We were certainly making the most of our trip out west. I continued to shoot roll after roll of film, capturing fantastic images of untamed rivers, vast deserts, and scores of majestic mountains spawned by glacial upheaval. I was in heaven, or at least in my mind, the next best thing to it.

Meanwhile, as we inched closer to California, John did a splendid job of keeping his lust for the stage in check. I wasn't sure if the exquisite scenery had distracted him from any anxieties he may have had or whether his inner confidence had just removed them altogether. Either way, he seemed more than eager to take on the comedy world. My grandfather told me a long time ago that the only things you attain in life are the things you really want. For John, there was no question; he wanted it badly. He was convinced that becoming a stand-up comedian wasn't just a whim; it was his destiny.

I can distinctly recall the sights and sounds of Los Angeles as if it were yesterday. The familiar sight of the infamous smog that everyone associates with L.A. was detectable but not as prominent as I had envisioned it to be. The temperature was in the midseventies accompanied by a mild breeze. The smell of the ocean was by far the most predominant scent, followed closely by a legion of food aromas that teased our palates. Towering palm trees dominated the landscape. Their numbers were only exceeded by the vast number of cars and interwoven highways that appeared to stretch on forever.

We made our way to Sunset Boulevard in search of a reasonably priced motel where John could establish a base for his attack on the comedy clubs. The Comedy Store was the first and most important club in his eyes. He had done his homework by arranging our arrival to coincide with amateur night at the Comedy Store. At the time, the Comedy Store was the Cadillac of comedy clubs. He was certain this club was the true litmus test as to whether or not he had what it took to hang with the heavyweights of comedy. Tonight's card featured several notable professionals that included the likes of Yakov Smirnoff, Sam Kennison, and a few others whom John knew, but I did not.

When we arrived at the Comedy Store, the atmosphere was electrically charged. Amateur night at the Comedy Store was unlike many of the other clubs who essentially offered an open mike to anyone who showed up. There were no guarantees that John would be allowed to perform. One first had to be selected among a field of aspiring comedians to gain the right to perform at the club. Earning this honor was no simple task. Looking over the place, I noticed a window that resembled something you'd see at a drive-through restaurant. John enlightened me on its purpose. Each comedian was required to register their act if they wished to be considered for selection. I watched as John stepped in line to sign up. Once he was registered, he was then placed in a pit that currently held about a dozen or so other comedians.

I can still vividly recall the scene. During the wait I began to size up the competition. I started laughing at the unusual array of concocted attires. I saw one guy dressed as a duck and another dressed in a psychedelic outfit that was sure to draw attention. I looked back at John to compare him with the rest of the field. John was wearing a jet-black suit with a bright white shirt. He also had on his trademark skinny black tie that featured piano keys traversing its length from top to bottom. For a final touch, he put gel in his hair for that slicked back look. It glistened in the fluorescent lighting of the pit. He looked good. Knowing how much it meant for John to get picked, I put in a special prayer for him.

While John remained in the pit, I could sense an increase in the already high level of energy in the air. Finally, the guy who had been given the power of selecting the hopefuls came forth with two other guys wearing Comedy Store T-shirts. I watched him scour the competition before making any decisions. After a few minutes he started selecting the contenders by pointing his finger at the chosen ones. Each time he picked someone, one of the guys who accompanied him pulled them from the pit. Several guys were taken while John remained in the pit. Things were getting very tense.

The next guy to be chosen was the guy in the psychedelic outfit. Then, to my relief, John was picked. I literally jumped for joy! I cheered as I watched him being led out of the pit by one of the roadies. It was truly a proud moment. Whether he succeeded or failed, his dream of getting a shot to perform at the biggest comedy club in Los Angeles was now a reality.

We split up at this point because only the performers were allowed backstage. I entered the establishment, paid the cover, and ordered a mixed drink. This cost me twenty bucks. On my budget, I was going have to nurse my ice-packed drink for as long as possible. Once the performers hit the stage, I laughed my way through several of the above-mentioned headliners before the amateurs were paraded out one by one. Two performers preceded John's act; one was good and one was not. When John came out, I think I was more nervous than he was. He put on a nearly flawless performance. The crowd gave him a rousing applause as he exited the stage. This and other performances that followed on this trip convinced him he had found his calling. His quest to become a stand-up comedian was no longer a dream. He was on his way.

When we returned home from our trip, he immediately began performing for a variety of venues. In the beginning his comedy performances were not always a raging success. As emcee for his act and co-writer for a good portion of his material, I saw firsthand the good, the bad, and the ugly. Undeterred, John kept at it, driven by the sound of applause. Within a short time poor performances became rare. His act was quickly becoming very polished.

I continued to be involved in his act. Writing comedy was by far my calling. We would sit around for hours combing through newspapers and magazines searching through real life stories on which we could put a comedic twist. I also incorporated my photography into his shows by shooting him in an array of humorous situations. The funniest of these scripted him as a lady's man on the prowl searching for seductive women. I took several different shots illustrating his various pick-up moves. One hilarious shot involved a cute girl pouring a pitcher of beer over his head after one of his advances had backfired. This was one of the beautiful things about working with John. If a situation had even the slightest hint of being funny, he was more than willing to pursue it with no regard for self-ridicule. His lack of inhibition allowed my creative juices to flow. I'm proud to say we made a pretty good team. Almost all of my comedy ideas became a mainstay in his act.

✝

As I sat next to him in his hospital room, we continued reliving many of the fond memories from his comedy career. We found great comfort in getting lost in those indelible memories. During these moments, I allowed myself to drift into a make-believe world where I could reverse time and undo everything that had happened so things were just as they were before I had ever left for Florida. These thoughts rapidly disintegrated when a knock on the door came from an orderly who was carrying my brother's dinner. I sat back and watched him force down a few bites. The sudden realization that our time together was coming to a swift end hit me like a ton of bricks. I can't ever remember feeling any sadder than in that moment. My heart told me I couldn't leave him to face his inevitable fate alone. Nothing could be more important than staying with him now. My brain reminded me that the reality of the situation was that this was our last night together. Later, worn out from all of our talking, he fell asleep. I remained by his side until I was forced to leave. I knew I was in for the longest night of my life.

When I returned to my room I could no longer hold back the tears that I had so dauntingly fought off while I was in his presence. I completely collapsed, sobbing uncontrollably. I was a mess. Each time I tried to face the facts of what was happening, I broke down worse than the time before. I kept trying to remind myself that I wasn't the one who was saddled with an incurable disease. The agonizing torment of being a witness to his slow decay exceeded any physical pain I had ever endured in my own life. Somehow I had to regain my composure; if not for me then at least for him. He knew what I was feeling. I didn't need to make it any harder on him.

Inside the dimly lit room I continued to weep as I prayed to God for a miracle. The utter hopelessness of it all was consuming me. I felt the desperation that goes along with a situation in which you have no control. I felt lost without hope. As I descended into a dark low, I became tormented by the things I had done and not done.

After the worst night's sleep I can ever recall, the morning finally arrived. I had already packed up what few belongings I had brought with me the night before. I skipped breakfast to make the most of what little time we had left together. Before entering his room, I had already begun to dread the thought that these moments would be our last together. Sensing the difficulty of what was to follow, I concocted a plan to distract us from the looming agony of saying goodbye. I had brought my camera with me, the same one that I had on our trip out west together. I told him I wanted to take some pictures of us together before I left. For obvious reasons he seemed reluctant at first, but eventually I was able to persuade him.

Over the years I had taken hundreds of pictures of my brother. It was hard for me to believe that these would be the last pictures I'd ever take of him. Despite the awkwardness of the moment, somehow the camera took some of the edge off our impending separation. As the minutes ticked by, the time for me to leave drew near. We could no longer prolong or dodge the emotional collapse. Tears flowed freely now. I held him tight, unsure of what to say. My final words to him were, "I love you." A few moments later, I was gone. It was the last time I saw him alive.

The plane that had taken me into the frozen, lifeless landscape of Iowa returned me to a wet, soggy, and inhospitable Florida. The overcast skies and torrential rains mirrored the dark mood into which I had settled. The dreadful weather symbolized the irreversible events yet to come. The waiting game had begun. For almost two years he battled his cancer with a ferocious determination. In the end he was unable to reclaim the life that was once his. I was now separated from him by over a thousand miles. I had never felt so alone in my life.

One night, shortly after I had come home from work, I received a call from his fiancée, Maria. Judging by the sound of her voice, I needed no further explanation to confirm my worst fears. As I listened in anticipation, she forced out the words I had refused to believe for so long. He was dying. She informed me he had slipped from consciousness into a deathly coma. The doctors were certain he had reached the end. Even though I knew it was coming, her words shredded me like a sickle cutting through dry brush. I was speechless when she uttered the words, "He's dying." Those words kept echoing through the hollow chamber of my mind. The reverberation refused to cease as I attempted to grapple with the reality of the situation.

The next thing I remember was Maria's voice telling me she was going to put the phone next to his ear so I could speak to him. After hearing this I somehow broke free from my catatonic state and began talking into the phone, knowing there would be no response. As awkward as this was, the words seem to flow from my heart. I told my brother I was sorry for letting him down. I told him I loved him with all of my strength and might. I promised him I would keep his memory alive with my children, and I would never forget how much he meant to me as a brother. As soon as these words had left my lips Maria returned to the phone, her quivering voice now inexplicably replaced with tearful excitement. She told me he had squeezed her hand in silent acknowledgment of the words I had just spoken. Crying openly she said, "Jim, he hears you! He hears you!" I felt a sudden warmth come over my body. Moved beyond words, I took great comfort in knowing he had heard me. It was more than I could have ever hoped for. Within several short moments he was gone; my only brother and best friend had died.

After an impossible night's sleep, I rose the next day still distraught over what had taken place the night before. I wasn't looking forward to calling my mother. I knew she would be equally if not more devastated than myself. Somehow I mustered the nerve to call her. Upon reaching her we immediately broke down and began crying. Her only question was if I would be able to return home for his funeral. I knew she needed me now more than ever. Somehow I had to find a way to get back. She was counting on me to carry out the difficult jobs of handling the extended family and facing the funeral procession.

I filled her in on my bleak financial situation. I promised her I would do my best to find a way to come up with the money. We talked over options, but there weren't many. She insisted I ask my father. He certainly had the means, but I knew he would never front me the money. Years of alcoholism had hardened his heart and numbed him from feeling much of anything for anyone. Receiving help from him was highly doubtful. Still, if my mother felt there was even a slim chance, I had to ask. When I finally called him for help his answer was swift and predictable. In his typical abrasive manner he told me, "You don't need to come home. He's already dead." His words echoed through my head just as Maria's had a couple of nights before. I should have known better than to let him destroy me in this way.

After his refusal I began racking my brain, desperately trying to come up with a way to get back. Then, out of nowhere, my father-in-law caught wind of my father's unwillingness to help. Joe was a good man. I had spent a lot of time helping him out around his farm. To say the least, when he offered to help, I was overjoyed by his gesture. I accepted his offer and thanked him many times over for saving the day. His only condition was that I pay him back as soon as I could, which in time, I did.

I've always heard, "Be careful what you wish for. You might just get it." Nothing could have been truer than the prospect of attending my brother's funeral. I knew I had to be there for my mother, his fiancée, and the family for support. However, I was not looking forward to the task that lay ahead. I did take comfort in knowing I would be with my family. I hoped they would give me strength in the same way they hoped I would strengthen them.

During my flight home I prayed for God to give me courage. The funeral was to take place in my hometown of Hanover, Illinois. The tiny village, tucked away in the northwestern corner of the state, is situated approximately thirty-five miles southeast of Dubuque, Iowa. During my recent trip to Iowa City, I had no means of transportation, so I was unable to visit my mother and sisters. Reuniting with them was something I definitely looked forward to.

I arrived home to a bittersweet welcome. Everyone was ecstatic to see me. However, John's passing brought forth a prevailing dark cloud that put a damper on everything. It was even tougher facing my brother's fiancée, Maria. Before ever leaving Dubuque, I had become close to Maria and her family. They had always treated me the same way they had treated John, with the utmost kindness. It was good that we had each other to lean on. It helped to lessen a heavy load.

The next day, my family, along with Maria's, entered the tiny funeral home where the wake took place. I felt drained even before it started. Somehow God gave me the strength to keep going. Confronting family and friends was by far the hardest part. Being reunited with so many faces from my past was extremely difficult under these circumstances. It's unfortunate when you reach a point in your life where it takes a funeral to reconnect with loved ones from your past.

As the line began to form, I took my position between my sister, Kerry, and Maria. As we greeted those in line I kept hearing the same words over again. Words like, "He's in a better place now," or "At least he's not suffering any longer." I couldn't help being angered by these comments. After all, who were they to sum things up? For some strange reason people feel compelled to fix your grief instead of sharing in it. A simple "I'm sorry," or "We're here for you," would have been so much better received. I knew they meant no disrespect, but I still felt hurt by their lack of empathy. Experience has taught me that those who are closest to death need time to accept their loss on their own terms. There is no silver bullet that can heal this kind of pain, only time. Even that's not a guaranteed fix.

The next day the automobile procession made the short trip to the local cemetery where my brother would be laid to rest. The funeral service was melancholy, everyone was dressed in black with heads bowed, their faces were sporting identical expressionless looks. The ceremony itself was brief. It didn't conclude until more tears had been shed. As I listened to the pastor's kind words, I felt a paralysis take hold of my body. I began to twitch involuntarily as the last words of the eulogy rang through my head. I could scarcely believe that my brother was being placed in the ground.

The motorcade departed from the cemetery with barely a sound. When the train of cars came to a stop during the trip back to the house, my mind immediately became absorbed with thoughts of him. How could it be possible? The reality that he was really gone was sinking in now.

I spent the rest of the day comforting my family and Maria. Maria stayed for a couple of hours before going back to Dubuque. Before leaving she presented me with a suitcase that I instantly recognized as John's. She told me it contained some of the clothes he had worn for his act as well as a few of the legendary props that had become his trademarks. She said it was only fitting that I should have it. I didn't have the courage to open it. My recent wounds had not even begun to heal, it would have to wait.

After saying goodbyes to my family, I flew out the next day. I returned home, relieved that the funeral was behind me. I knew the days that lay ahead were not going to be easy. I tried to accept what had happened, but the harder I tried to put it behind me the worse it got. I couldn't get the visual picture of his withered body out of my head. I kept seeing the disappointment on his face when I failed to honor his dying request to bring Tyler along for our final visit. I would now have to live with that for the rest of my life. I had let him down in so many ways.

The irreparable finality of it all was slowly tearing me apart. I was dangling on the precipice of unstableness. Time became my enemy. Each day the deep wound in my soul opened up a little bit further. My nature became self-destructive. In a sorry attempt to put my troubles behind me, I resorted to drinking heavily. My choice of poison mattered not. Essentially, my goal was simple: escape reality as quickly as possible. Having never been much of a drinker, this practice quickly began to take a toll on my physical and mental health. I stopped attending church as I wrestled with the various stages of grief. I had no interest in facing my brave new world without my brother. I never felt so alone in my life. My brother had always been there for me, encouraging me to forge ahead, regardless if things looked bleak. Life suddenly didn't seem worth living. I even entertained suicide, but deep down inside I knew I lacked the courage, or should I say the cowardice. I kept thinking he was looking down on me. This was the one thing that kept me going.

A couple of weeks passed as I remained imprisoned in a self-condemned, vegetative state. One day, for some unknown reason, I remembered the suitcase Maria had given me. I decided I had waited long enough to open it. I had put the suitcase in a small closet in my room where it had remained since I returned home from the funeral. After retrieving it from the closet, I brought it into my living room and placed it on my couch. I took a few moments before opening it, contemplating whether or not this was a good idea. Curiosity won out. I slowly popped the latches on each side of the case. It was so full it burst open like a jack-in-the-box. I gazed at its contents for a few moments. A rush of memories hit me like a tidal wave.

The first item in the case was a denim jacket he had worn for many of his informal shows. As I pulled it out of the suitcase

I could smell his scent on it. After slowly digesting this recollection, I set the jacket aside. Underneath the jacket were a few more articles of his clothing. Among these items was his famous piano key tie that he had worn to practically every important show in which he had performed. Below the clothes I found a cache of props that defined his comedic style. Among these items was a bundle of dynamite sticks attached to a wooden plunger, a blond wig, and perhaps his most famous prop, a speculum that had a mustache and glasses attached to it. I laughed out loud when I saw it. He frequently used it in his act as a quasi-ventriloquist, where he would open and close the speculum as if it were talking. He would often point it in the direction of a female in the crowd and say, "Who's your friend?"

It didn't take long before the fond memories led me back to his death. The laughs suddenly turned into tears. Too painful to continue, I quickly shoved everything back into the case. I tried to close it, but there was just too much stuff. Wanting to rid myself of it for the moment, I set it back in the closet halfway open. I told myself I'd close it later when I wasn't so emotionally drained.

That incident provoked me into a heavy night of drinking. During this time, the house we lived in was very small. It had only two bedrooms. Because of this, my son Tyler slept in my room on a spare bed in front of the same closet where I kept the suitcase. South Florida was notorious for burglaries. Almost every house had standard-issue bars across the windows to deter any would-be intruders. There were only two doors that entered the house. Each of these was equipped with a series of deadbolts I routinely secured each night before going to bed. After drinking myself silly, I locked the house down and went to bed.

Sometime during the middle of the night, I awoke from a dead sleep. I popped my head up in a half-conscious state and became startled when I noticed a figure standing at the end of my son's bed staring directly at him while he slept. Still woozy from the booze, my head slumped back on my pillow. I tried to tell myself I must have imagined it, but something I saw bothered me. When I had raised my head, I noticed the figure methodically glance over at me to acknowledge me awaking, but then, undeterred, it nonchalantly turned its full attention back on my son. Judging by the size of the figure, I knew it had to be a man. My mind began to race as I quickly retraced the moments before I went to bed. I knew I had secured all the deadbolts, but somehow, someone had violated the security of my home. Convinced of what I had just seen, I knew I had to confront the intruder.

In one motion I popped my head up and looked directly at the figure, but before I could get a clear fix, the figure transformed into a ghost-like apparition right before my very eyes. Then, what remained darted into my closet at lightning speed, leaving nothing behind but a vapor trail. I rubbed my eyes, wondering if what I had just seen was real. I immediately thought of the suitcase. I rationalized that somehow it provided a medium that permitted John's spirit to come forth. Something inside told me it was him. I was convinced he had come back, refusing to be denied of seeing his nephew one last time. It was the only explanation I could come up with. I decided right then and there to never tell anyone about this experience, for surely no one would believe me; or, worse yet, I'd be accused of completely losing my marbles.

The next morning I awoke to my son jumping on top of me in my bed. He looked me square in the eyes and asked me if I'd seen the man in our room last night. As he uttered these words, the hair on the back of my neck stood straight up. A chill ran up and down my spine. Mortified, I simply replied, "You saw him too?" My son told me he saw a man standing at the foot of his bed staring intently at him. Too frightened to open his eyes fully, he kept them squinted, hoping the figure didn't notice he was awake. I confessed to my son I had seen the figure as well. I told him I was certain it was his uncle who had returned from the afterlife to see him one last time. To further ease Tyler's conscience, we conducted a full inspection of the house, checking for any signs of a forced entry. We found all of the deadbolts still in place. This helped both of us to accept my theory.

Now one would think that such an experience would render one's doubts as to the validity of the afterlife. Despite this incredible experience, it still failed to dislodge the guilt that was deeply imbedded in my soul. Badgered by my neglectfulness during my brother's terrible ordeal, I remained tormented by the fact I had let him down when he needed me most.

A few nights later, I had an incredible dream. It was so real I couldn't tell if I was dreaming or not. There I was driving my car, when I happened to glance over at the passenger's side and to my complete astonishment, I saw my brother sitting right next to me. I was immediately taken back by seeing him but was even more shocked by his appearance. Incredibly, he looked better than I had ever seen him when he was alive. His body was literally glowing. I was practically speechless as I laid eyes on him. When I finally gathered my senses, I looked at him and said, "John, are you all right?" He looked over at me and smiled. He then said, "Of course I'm all right. Now I want you to get on with your life. You have so much to live for, and if things were reversed, you wouldn't want me moping around feeling sorry for you, would you?" I answered him by shaking my head no. I then reached out to touch him, but he disappeared. It was then that I awoke from my dream. I was so disoriented that I wasn't sure if he had died at all. After a few more seconds passed by, I finally realized I had been dreaming.

The experience was so real I was convinced it was more of a visit than a dream. By no stretch of the imagination was I healed from my loss, but the dream did serve as a wake-up call, reminding me that feeling sorry for myself was no longer an option. This wasn't my first encounter with tragic loss, nor would it be the last, but in order to appreciate the full story, we must go back to the beginning, back to where it all began.

Humble Beginnings

My story begins in the early 1960s. It takes place in Hanover, Illinois, a small Midwestern town located along the upper northwestern corner in the state of Illinois. The family is comprised of nine members, my father, George, my mother, Josephine, five children, John, Kerry, Eydie, Jim (yours truly), Sara, and my grandparents, Orma and Sarah, who lived next door to us. Much like the television show, *The Waltons,* the children shared a symbiotic relationship with their grandparents that never wavered during their time together. Unlike *The Waltons,* my immediate family seldom, if ever, functioned as a family unit. From early on something was distinctly wrong with my family. Our days were filled with tension and fighting, accompanied by an ever-present fear that remained a constant throughout my childhood. The source of that fear was my father, whose actions severed all possibilities of normality and plunged my family into the deep abyss of dysfunctional living.

During my childhood years, we had no conception of what was normal. Therefore, we believed my father's continual outrages were something all families experienced. My initial perceptions of my family could be best described where each of us were situated on the family totem pole. Unfortunately for me, since I was the fourth child in the family, I was positioned in an unenviable spot for a number of reasons. The first being that I was the second son, who, being "second stew" so to speak, received less attention than my older brother. In retrospect, I came to realize this was actually a blessing. The second reason was that I was one of the youngest children but not the baby, who we all know typically receives a great deal more attention than those who are older. The third reason was I was the second middle child, thus putting me one step below the oft-overlooked middle child. In reality, it really didn't matter where you were located on this pole, just being on the pole meant you were in for a rough ride.

Grandpa and Grandma Winter

My grandparents lived directly next door to us and were quite the opposite of my parents. Despite the fact that their means were modest, they somehow managed to have just about every creature comfort that couples strive to obtain. This included a big house, new cars, and all the amenities associated with a good home life. Many people in our town regarded them as "pillars of the community." They attained this stature through their good citizenship, high moral conduct, and above all, an outward commitment to spiritual values. To many, they defined the term *wholesomeness*.

My grandfather was gifted with immense wisdom. He held a seat on the town board for many years. Seldom was a decision made before consulting him. Slow to judge and slow to anger, he would approach problems first and foremost with prayer, and then and only then, would he pursue solutions. He believed that God guided his every word and deed. When praise came, he never basked in it. Instead, he exhibited humility by giving God the credit.

If you were looking from the outside in, it would be easy to surmise that his life was simple, yet a closer look revealed an extremely complex human being, who in my opinion, was the closet thing to spiritual perfection I have ever seen. According to my mother, he was the go-to source whenever the township sought sound advice. His wisdom was so crystal clear that you would have thought he possessed a magic window to peer into either the past or future and retrieve whatever knowledge was necessary to solve the problem at hand. Insightfulness was just one of his many qualities.

My grandparents were devout members of the United Methodist church. My parents, on the other hand, seldom attended church. My mother told me the reason for this was that my father had a falling out with some of the church elders. Evidently one Sunday they confronted him over the amount of his offering, or should I say the lack thereof. Naturally he was offended by their assessments and subsequently stopped participating altogether. When my grandfather caught wind that my father had severed all ties to the church, he promptly came over to our house to confront my father on the matter. The last thing I recall him saying was, "If you're not going to take these kids to church, then we are." From that moment forward, a new ritual began where every Sunday morning our grandparents would pull their big Buick up in front of our house and all five kids would pile in to make the three-block journey to receive our spiritual fulfillment, and then, immediately afterward, they returned us to our dysfunctional home life. I came to refer to this paradox as my "baptism by toilet water."

Our home life was the furthest thing from a Christian home; yet, right next door lived our grandparents who modeled the Christian experience. They were the spiritual paragons we so desperately needed. Not only did they take it upon themselves to ensure we attended church regularly, they also took time out of their busy lives to enlighten us on the teachings of the Scriptures. Gradually over time we learned there was another way to lead your life. Unfortunately, as long as our father remained in the picture, there was no hope for our family to even remotely resemble this other way to live your life. Through the years our grandparents' home served as a sanctuary, sparing us from my father's wrath innumerable times. Despite this haven we knew we were trapped, for even though we could see paradise from our fence, at best we could only visit it from time to time.

For the majority of our childhood my parents never owned a car, or for that matter a phone, until almost all of us were fully grown. My father managed to get to and from work by carpooling for years. He didn't seem to mind being deprived of these fundamental necessities that most families took for granted. However, the rest of us who lived with him felt trapped in a bubble of isolation that left us devoid of almost all outside contact with the rest of the free world. It was reminiscent of the Iron Curtain that descended over Eastern Europe at the close of World War II, whereby my father played the role of Joseph Stalin while the rest of our family represented the helpless citizens of Eastern Europe. I'm sure that comparing my father to Stalin must sound a little harsh. Unfortunately, it wasn't that far from the truth. It was obvious to all of us that he was not a happy person. He seemed to be mad at the world, but no one knew why. In time, it became clear that the source of his tyrannical disposition was his addiction to alcohol. The more he drank the more abusive he became. After years of alcoholism, he ultimately became a slave to the power it held over him, which sealed our fates along with his. This road of no return became a living hell for us. As long as we lived within the four walls of what we called home, any hopes for normalcy would remain fleeting.

It wasn't long before we were at the complete mercy of his incessant tormenting. The only breaks in this vicious cycle came when he was so drunk that he had neither the strength nor the mental capacity for dishing it out. We were the poster children for a dysfunctional family.

In the years that followed we were literally slammed back and forth in the same way a tennis ball is volleyed across a net, never fully knowing which side of the two contrasting lifestyles we would end up on.

Our grandparents were truly our saving grace. They married in their early twenties and went on to raise three sons, an adopted daughter, and numerous foster children. My grandmother's maiden name was Turner. Her descendents were primarily of English and Scottish descent. Sarah, who was called Sally by everyone who knew her, could only be described as intense. Even though her blonde hair had turned snow white, the curls from her youth remained. Despite her advanced years, the fire in her eyes still burned brightly. But above everything, it was her righteous resolve with all things that defined who she was.

According to my grandmother, we had royal blood flowing through our veins. Supposedly there was a duke who originated from her side of the family. She continually reminded us to be mindful of our heritage by conducting ourselves with the same dignity as our chivalrous ancestors. I admired her approach of not allowing anything to devalue herself, regardless of the circumstances. It was something we could relate to in our own lives. She always said, "No matter how bad things get, resist taking the easy way out.–Never compromise your values, and never forget who you are and where you came from."

Sarah was a strong-spirited woman who knew her ideals and led her life in accordance with them. She was an accomplished poet, owned and operated a successful business of baking wedding cakes, and feared nothing but the Creator. Unquestionably she was the matriarch of her extended family. To set the record straight, the respect she received from her family was partly out of fear, but no one could refute her high standards of moral conduct. She didn't just preach what she taught; she lived it with conviction.

My grandfather, George, who went by his middle name Orma, was the fourth of six children. He preferred to be called Orm for short. Supposedly, his parents were unsettled on a middle name until they saw the name Orma on the stove they owned. They liked it, and the rest is history. The Winters were primarily of German descent, and they immigrated to the United States during the early 1800s.

To me, my grandfather is the greatest man I have ever known. Orm was a big, stout, man who stood six-foot two. His latter years failed to diminish his strong jawbone and chiseled good looks. His greatest physical feature was the naturally relaxed, almost jovial expression he wore on his face. It made him extremely approachable. He treated me like a son and I looked up to him as if he were my father. I drew close to him at an early age, no doubt attracted by his impeccable character.

Early in his life my grandfather worked at the local woolen mill. He later became a civil defense worker for the government, and in his retirement years he was the sexton for the townships' cemeteries.

My grandfather's work resume hardly seems fitting for someone who would be associated with greatness. However, as I have come to learn over time, jobs and income are not what makes one great. For quite some time I had difficulty understanding how my grandfather lived beyond his apparent means. He once told me that it's not how much you make, it's what you do with what you make. I remember him telling me his starting wage from his first job at the woolen mill was a mere thirteen cents an hour. There's little doubt that these humble beginnings equipped him with a conservative approach to life. As time went on, he remained loyal to his conservative ways, eventually saving enough money to acquire four plots of land with a house that was located in the center of town. He maintained a garden in his backyard to help supplement the need for food. Gardening would become a lifelong passion of his that would ultimately be handed down to his son and, in a much more limited respect, to his grandchildren as well.

During the prime of his life he worked at the Savanna Army Depot. Known to locals as "the depot," it was a high-security military installation that was a major employer for the entire county prior to the outbreak of World War II. The depot was a production facility and proving ground for various types of explosive materials that ultimately played a vital role in the upcoming wars in which America became engaged. Strategically located in a heavily wooded section along the Mississippi River, the site provided seclusion from the general public and more importantly offered an ideal access to river and railroad transportation. The jobs at the depot were physically challenging, not to mention dangerous. Men worked on long magazines handling an assortment of highly volatile materials. These munitions were used to thwart the evil ambitions of Hitler and the Axis powers. It was not uncommon to hear stories of men getting their heads blown off or losing a limb. Yes, working at the depot was definitely high risk, but for the men who worked there, it was more than just a source of income. Many, including my grandfather, viewed their work as an act of patriotism.

The twilight of my grandfather's life was spent as the local sexton for the town's cemeteries, where his duties ranged from selling headstones, grave digging, and mowing the acreage of the three cemeteries that were under the town's supervision. Again, not the kind of life that one looking from the outside in would associate with greatness. However, looks can be deceiving.

There was a certain calmness about my grandfather. He possessed an inner peace that few men experience. He relied on humility and simplicity to bypass the temptations that most of us wrestle with day in and day out. These innate qualities were seemingly God given. I mentioned earlier that when he bought his home he purchased two additional lots of land. This was a classic example of his insightfulness. He always had a plan. He knew a good thing when he saw it, and he wasn't afraid to act on it. Whether he knew what he'd do with the additional plots or not, his savvy business decisions had a certainty about them when one considers the lean times in which he lived. I'm sure he would have credited his Maker for this talent as well.

A short time after their marriage, my grandparents started a family. During the 1930s they would have three sons, George, my father, and John and Jim, for whom my brother and I were named after. As mentioned earlier, they adopted a girl named Kay and were also foster parents for numerous children through the years.

Dear Old Dad

During the early 1950s, my grandparents children came of age. My father was the oldest of the three boys. He, like his brother John, entered the service after their high school graduation. Jim, the youngest brother, went on to college, got a degree, and became a schoolteacher. Later on he earned his master's. In between his academic pursuits he married and fathered a son. In the latter stages of his life he became a successful businessman. John, after serving his time in the military, returned home from the army. He married and, like his father, raised three sons. Like his younger brother Jim, he obtained a degree and acquired his master's as well. John worked several different jobs at the same time for many years. He enjoyed success in all of them.

When my father completed his military obligation, he returned home. With the help of my grandfather, he acquired a position at the Savanna Army Depot. This would become his life's work.

Fast-forward to 1960, the year of my birth. My grandfather gave my father the two additional lots he had purchased years before so he could build a home for his growing family. It's important to acknowledge the immense impact my grandfather had on his children and grandchildren. He was much more than just a father figure. He championed the positive role model yet never sought any recognition nor boasted about doing it. Herein laid the beauty of the man. He always prioritized God and family first and foremost. He possessed that rare unselfish quality of resisting secular pleasures for the sake of staying in accordance to the teachings of the Bible. He followed its moral code implicitly. This is significant because when most of us read the Bible, we find that comprehending it and living it are two entirely different things. My grandfather was able to do the latter, and he did it with conviction. His devotion to the Lord and the Word inspired me to unravel the enigma of why he was so committed to this life of unconditional faith to God.

My father was an extremely intelligent fellow, but he displayed no spiritual qualities. His intelligence brought him some noteworthy achievements such as a well-paid job and eventually high-ranking status at the depot. Later in his career he worked on top-secret projects involving the construction of atomic weapons. After I learned of his involvement with the nuclear program, I wondered if maybe the pressures from this type of work were responsible for his lifelong battle with alcoholism. I found history would suggest otherwise.

From an early age my father had the reputation of being a "hard ass." As the oldest, he did his best to secure his authority. He leveraged his age and size to establish dominion over his younger brothers, making sure he vanquished any resistance either of them may have given. However, he underestimated the brothers who ultimately combined forces to even the sides. After succumbing to my father a few times, they secretly plotted a surprise attack that he failed to see coming.

The incident unfolded while all three brothers were at the top of the stairs at my grandparents' home. Within a few moments the three of them were at the bottom of the stairs with my dad crashing into a bushel of apples, his brothers on top of him making sure they'd finished the job. My grandfather remained neutral as he idly sat by reading his newspaper. By now my father was pleading in vain for his rescue. This was a classic example of my grandfather's wisdom. By not taking action, he allowed the scene to unfold. In doing so, he taught his children to work out their own problems while at the same time making sure my father had learned his lesson. Suddenly the tables had turned. My father was forced to respect his brothers whether he liked it or not, and for the time being, the powers at hand were balanced. His brothers had earned his respect the hard way, and my father realized he could no longer simply force his will on them.

Unfortunately this did not prevent him from forcing his will on himself. By the time he was fifteen, my father was caught with hard liquor in his bedroom. Knowing my grandparents and their high moral standards, I would have loved to have been a fly on the wall when this went down. This incident marks the origin of my father's lifelong battle with alcoholism.

My father elected to forego college. This resulted in him being drafted in the United States Army shortly before the outbreak of the Korean War. One can only imagine the feelings of a firstborn son going off to a strange land at a dangerous time. Much like the young men and women of our armed forces today, it can be disturbing to see how history repeats itself. My father was located in what was known as the "Three Point Area" (close to where the fighting was going on), but managed to avoid combat when his musical talents were discovered. He definitely had a gift with music. He played the saxophone, clarinet, French horn, and the piano. On top of that he could play almost any of the popular tunes of the day without the aid of a musical score. He was soon performing for field hospitals and playing backup music for USO shows. It is not known whether or not my father's drinking accelerated from his military experience in Korea. Odds are it did. Despite being spared from combat, I'm sure he witnessed many of the horrible things that accompany the carnage of war.

After my father returned home from Korea, he met my mother and soon after they were married. My earliest memories of my father's devotion to the beer can came in the form of photographs that he had taken of him and his buddies doing some heavy drinking in the great outdoors. My father developed an interest in photography during his years of military service in Korea. While in Korea, he purchased a 35 mm camera. He took many splendid shots of the Korean countryside and its people. When he returned home, he continued to take pictures.

One day, I discovered a pile of his photos he had left out on the kitchen table. I began thumbing through them with mild curiosity. As I viewed the photos I became fascinated at how a photograph could actually capture time. It sparked something within me, and before long, I wanted a camera of my own to show people my view of the world.

I made my dream come true when I spotted an offer for a camera on a Bazooka bubble gum wrapper. It was a primitive black and white 110 camera, but it could be mine if I saved twenty-five wrappers and a dollar. I soon went on a mission collecting bubble gum wrappers while saving every penny I could get my hands on. Before long the camera was mine. The image quality of the pictures it took was extremely poor. It ended up breaking after a few rolls of film, but nevertheless it served its purpose by fueling an interest that would become a lifelong passion.

While thumbing through more of my father's pictures, I noticed the familiar Hamm's beer can was ever present with its bright blue triangular emblems cascading up and down the sides of the can highlighted by those indelible words inscribed across the bottom, "Born in the land of sky blue waters." This slogan became a fixture in our home as well as in his photos.

Interestingly enough, within this collection of inebriated depictions, I found many photos of the beautiful surrounding countryside of Jo Daviess County. One photo in particular that caught my eye stood out from the rest. It was a picture of a gigantic cottonwood tree. In front of this monstrosity stood my father and an entourage of his beer-drinking buddies partaking in an afternoon barbeque. In unison with steady grips they hoisted their Hamm's beer cans high in the air while making a celebratory toast. The width of this tree had to measure at least twelve feet across and twenty-five feet in circumference. The sheer enormity of this massive creation instantaneously captured my imagination, filling me with a respect for nature. As I viewed the photo, I stood in silent awe at how such a magnificent life form could have arisen from a mere sapling. I couldn't help but wonder if it could speak what stories it could tell! This was truly no ordinary tree. I became obsessed with the photo. I was determined to find out more about this tree.

Somehow, my raging curiosity gave me the courage to ask my dad if he could tell me its exact location. When I prodded him for information about the tree, he scowled at me and said, "Never mind about that tree. It's no place for kids!" The stern tone of his reply signaled an abrupt end to my questioning. If I was going to find out anything about the tree, I would have to do it on my own. From here on, old trees held a certain fascination over me.

Some years later I remember reading about "The Judgment Tree" in the stories of Daniel Boone. The Judgment Tree was an enormous tree under which Boone and his newfound countrymen would gather on a regular basis to solve disputes. Boone himself served as the ruling judge, and as I read the story I couldn't help but think of the powerful symbolism at work here. The age of the tree clearly stood for wisdom while its sheer size represented strength and stability. As I continued to read about "The Judgment Tree," I couldn't help but draw comparisons to "The Tree." I'm not sure if anyone actually named the tree "The Tree," but those who knew of it just seemed to refer to it in this manner. Simple, yet profound; I couldn't help but think of how appropriate this designation was!

After I had graduated from high school and moved away from home, I would occasionally return to Hanover to see the family. During my visits I would question some of the old timers who had spent most of their lives there to see if they knew the exact location of "the tree." Most people agreed that the tree was located roughly ten miles southwest of Hanover, but none of them could pinpoint its precise location. During one of those return trips I came across an old timer who knew of the tree. He informed me it had fallen from old age a few years back. I sat stoically as the words rolled off his tongue, trying not to show my disappointment. Like so many things in my life, it just wasn't in the cards. As time went on, I never forgot the tree and how a photo stirred me to a lifelong passion for nature. It was easy for me to understand my father's love for photography, but I never understood his love for alcohol and what it did to him.

On the surface most people would agree that beer is less harmful than hard liquor, and from my own personal experience, I would have to agree. The big difference here was not so much the choice of poison but rather the rate at which it was consumed. My dad was seldom seen without a can of beer firmly gripped in his hand. Whenever he had any free time away from work, it became fair game for his favorite pastime.

He consumed beer and became consumed by beer, which was without question the major focus of his life. The only exception to this lifelong vice was "the garden." Each spring he leased a small parcel of land where he could grow some vegetables. It proved to be one of the few redeeming qualities he would inherit from his father. Unfortunately, it failed to diminish his love for the beer can, which in time evolved into a devouring addiction for him and a dreaded curse for the rest of the family.

A Beer Garden of a Most Unusual Variety

A few years after our home was built, my father ventured into a business deal with five other men to purchase some land in the country so he could have a garden he could truly call his own. I will say this about the garden. Its sheer size rivaled any garden I have ever seen. It was easily more than two acres in size and contained every kind of vegetable imaginable. He even grew his own spices. The surplus easily fed our family as well as many others, but not without a price. My poor mother spent years of her life enslaved to canning and preserving every spoil his garden yielded, only for the majority of it to be given away.

As a child I can distinctly recall that whenever the word *garden* was mentioned, it was like a religious experience. For my father, it was as if doves were descending from heaven at precisely the same moment the word *garden* was spoken. The garden was the final frontier, a place where no kid wanted to go. I was such a kid. Since we lived in town and didn't own a car, my dad had to rely on my grandfather to transport him and me to and from the garden. The three of us, each representing a different generation, embarked on this daily ritual that lasted for years.

It wasn't all bad, for it gave me an opportunity to experience something other than the confines of my own yard. The garden was located roughly five miles outside of town. Its allure held a mystical grip over each of us in its own unique way.

To my grandfather, the garden was a means of handing down the traditions of past generations. His endless devotion to working the land ensured a strong harvest. It also gave the garden its pristine look.

To my father, the garden was the one place other than the tavern where he truly felt at peace with himself. He could now chase his dream of growing the best vegetables known to mankind. He had done his homework by selecting the best seeds available. The land he purchased provided ample quantities of rich black soil. Together, these ingredients formed an unbeatable combination for gardening glory. If only he could have treated his family half as well as he did the soil. Instead he chose to treat us like dirt.

For me, the garden initially felt like a prison in which I was held captive in a dim world where pulling weeds and planting seeds were the highlight of my day. Later on though, I came to cherish my days at the garden, for it was priceless time spent with my grandfather. He opened my eyes to the natural beauty of the surrounding countryside, furthering my growing interest with nature and photography.

My grandfather taught me many things about the great outdoors. The most important of these lessons was learning how to slow down enough to listen for the sounds of nature. Among these melodious sounds was a symphony of birds each singing a different song. I discovered insects of every shape, color, and size twitching, chirping, and buzzing by as they went about their business. He made me recognize the resounding northerly and southerly winds as they rustled the leaves of the trees and how, in conjunction with the sounds of the fauna, it created a rhapsody of nature.

Then there was that one distinct sound I could always count on like clockwork: my father cracking open a frosty Hamm's beer can at seven o'clock in the morning. On one such occasion I can recall one of my dad's gardening buddies pulling up the lane to our garden while my father was in the process of opening a beer. When he witnessed my father drinking a beer at such an early hour, he shouted out in a loud voice, "Frosty!" (That had been my dad's nickname for as long as I could remember. Get it? "Frosty" Winter. Now, he knew my father's affinity for the beer can, but even he was astonished to see him slurping one down at seven a.m.!) In a concerned voice he remarked, "For crying out loud, Frosty, why don't you drink some water? There's plenty of it over there in those barrels." Without the slightest hesitation my dad fired back a reply, "I'm saving the water for the plants!" I thought to myself, *Such consideration, and such concern!* I was truly dumbfounded by his lightning-quick response and the ease with which he justified his twisted love for the golden elixir. It was a shame that his family would never receive such thoughtfulness.

To this day the words *beer garden* take on a different meaning for me. The garden always came first over us kids. The garden always got Lorsban 15 (a favorite pesticide of my father) before we received adequate clothing. I can clearly recall having only one or two pairs of blue jeans whose knees were so knocked out and fitted so tightly that the button that fastened them kept popping out every time I bent over. This predicament led to an embarrassing incident that occurred in our front yard. An old war buddy of my dad's happened to stop by to say hello. As they conversed, my father noticed his buddy staring at my grass-stained knees and popped-opened jeans. In an attempt to justify my pathetic appearance, my father quickly scolded me by saying, "How in the hell am I going to keep you in pants?" My first instinct was to say, "You haven't bought me a pair in two years," but the fear of a right cross kept me silent.

He then proceeded to tell his buddy an old joke about a country boy whose jeans kept popping open every time he sat down to eat at the dinner table. He told the joke with a strong Southern accent and it went something like this, "Ma? What, Pa? When are we gonna get that boy a new pair of blue jeans? Well how's come, Pa? 'Cause that's the third time this week he's drug his pecker through the mashed potaters!" They enjoyed a hearty laugh at my expense. Such was his way in life, denying reality so he could save face. This event, like so many others, wreaked havoc on my self-esteem. It would take years for me to rise above it.

Further testament of my father's selfish nature came when he chose to purchase a ground tiller instead of a car for his growing family. In his eyes the needs of the garden far outweighed the needs of his family. He reasoned that his garden was too big not to have one, and besides, the family had survived this long without a car, surely they could survive a little longer. The big question was how he intended to transport the tiller to and from the garden. It was too large to fit in the cab of my grandfather's truck. It appeared he had the cart before the horse. It was then that he came up with a scheme. He reasoned if he could get the tiller out to the garden, he could leave it there, thus eliminating the need for a vehicle to haul it to and fro. He arranged for one of his beer-drinking buddies to get it out to the garden and the problem was solved. It was further proof of how my family was held hostage by a rogue gardener.

With the acquisition of the tiller, he had taken a huge step toward his quest of becoming the king of gardeners. He gained further momentum by generously sharing his bounty with the local circle of gardeners. What better way was there than to have the local competition talking up the spoils of his toil. After gaining the respect of the immediate community, he expanded his notoriety by writing a series of articles for some of the local papers. The articles were packed with tips on how to plant and grow superior vegetables, not to mention a few of his personal trade secrets thrown in for good measure. Eventually these publications caught the eye of the horticulturists at the University of Illinois. It wasn't long after that he completed his journey to gardening glory when he was appointed Master Gardner for the State of Illinois. This designation was truly an amazing accomplishment. In the gardening community he was the envy of the county. We all had to take our hats off to him. I personally took pride in his appointment because I played a hand in the garden's success. I still have a modest garden today. When I'm working in it, I can't help but think back to those unforgettable days of the garden.

Mom

My mother, Josephine, whose maiden name was Heim, went by the name of Jo Ann. She married my father shortly after his return from the Korean War. She would bear four children in five years, or in other words, she essentially remained pregnant from 1955 to 1960. My youngest sister Sara topped off the load when she arrived in 1963. Throughout most of my life I found myself in an ongoing state of pity for my mother. Through the years many of my relatives reminded me I shouldn't feel sorry for her because, after all, she made the decision to stay with my father. Although this was true, like most good sons, I didn't care what kind of decisions my mother had made in the past or what mistakes she continued to make in the present. I simply loved her and wanted nothing but the best for her. Those who were on the outside looking in were only seeing part of the picture.

When my mother entered into matrimony, she believed in her vows for richer or poorer, for better or worse, in sickness and in health, and so forth. People didn't just go around divorcing each other like they do today. In my mother's case, she had more than enough viable reasons to seek a divorce. There was the physical and mental abuse, the depravity, and worst of all, the nightmare of being married to an alcoholic. I've often wondered how difficult it must have been for her to come to terms with the reality that the person she married was not who she thought he was, especially after conceiving five children. Most of us who have been married would agree that marriage is a process requiring ongoing effort from both parties.

They say love can cross over all boundaries. Nothing validates this statement more succinctly than the marriage of my parents. For the entire duration of their marriage, my father deprived my mother of even the simplest of comforts. Without question the burden of their marriage rested squarely on the shoulders of funding his insatiable alcoholic thirst which put an enormous strain on the family budget. His tight-fisted grip on the finances left the rest of his family virtually destitute.

My mother accepted these harsh conditions with little resistance. She was definitely not a materialistic person, but the sacrifices she made were often extreme, such as going years on only one pair of shoes or saving pennies just so her children could experience the simple pleasure of a candy bar. Whenever she gave me money I felt guilty, knowing deep down inside there was no treat for her. This illustrates how she sacrificed everything for us, right down to the most basic indulgences that life had to offer. Looking back on it now, it seems unfathomable as to how or why anyone would subject themselves to a life such as this. I knew firsthand of my father's domineering nature and how each of us submitted to it or faced the consequences of his terrible wrath. I concluded she was prey to the same fate as the rest of us.

I loved my mother more than anything in the world. She had a heart of gold, and we knew she was always in our corner. She wasn't a strong woman in terms of sticking her neck out for what she believed in. I'm sure this was primarily due to living in the shadow of my father. Despite being beaten down over the years, she never ceased supporting her children. She did her best to build each of us up in whatever way she could. She would tell me things like I was her favorite child, but if I ever repeated it, she would deny it wholly. Maybe she told each of us the same thing. I'll never know and it really wasn't important. What was important was that she loved each of her children unconditionally, and that love was incapable of being extinguished, even by our father.

Mom's Side of the Family

As to her life before my father, much less is known of my mother's side of the family, simply due to lack of contact. She was born and raised in Galena, Illinois. When she was first married to my father, the majority of her immediate family still lived there. Galena was only a half hour's drive away, but when you don't own a car, even a short distance seemed like an eternity away.

My mother's childhood was relatively normal from the standpoint that she had a set of parents who loved and cared for her. Her father's name was Joe and her mother's name was Cecilia. Ceil, as she was affectionately referred to, passed away while my mother was still carrying me, so I have no memory of her at all. My mother was in her late twenties when Ceil died, and because of the tragic circumstances surrounding her death, Mom seldom spoke of her. I know she was deeply moved by her sudden death, and I am convinced it added to her submissive nature in regard to my father.

Her father, Joe, who was quite a few years older than his wife Ceil, remained a widower after her passing. He owned a shop on Main Street in Galena, and I can remember visiting him when I was a young lad. The visits are still vivid in my mind because of a certain box of wooden toy soldiers he kept in the bottom drawer of an old beat-up cabinet. To a young deprived boy, playing with toy soldiers was about as good as it got. Those were fond memories.

When I was eight years old, Joe died suddenly from an apparent heart attack. This was my first encounter with death. I can distinctly recall my father summoning the family into the living room to announce that Grandpa Joe had passed away. He told us in a very matter-of-fact way that seemed insensitive for the seriousness of the moment. For the first time in my life, I contemplated death and felt the sorrow that's associated when losing someone you've cared for. My mother was distraught and suddenly parentless. I can still see the pain on her face. It still saddens me when I think of it.

My knowledge of my mother's childhood is sketchy at best. She was born a twin, but her brother died a few months after birth. She also had an older brother and a younger sister. Her older brother, Donald, enlisted in the army shortly after he graduated from high school. He ended up making the army his career. He eventually married, had a family, and settled down in California. He did return home to visit his family through the years, but my memories of him have always been foggy.

Her sister Rosie was the youngest of the three. She married a fine man from nearby Stockton, Illinois, who, like her brother, was also named Donald. He became more affectionately known as Bing, possibly to avoid confusion with his wife's brother. Rosie and Bing were very much in love. They had one child, a boy named Steven.

Rosie and her family were pretty much the sole representation of the Heim side of the family while we were growing up. Over the years we spent quite a few afternoons visiting them at their home in Galena. This was made possible by my grandparents, who made weekly pilgrimages to Dubuque, Iowa, to do their shopping. Since Galena was on the way, they generously allowed my mother and us grandchildren to hitch a ride so we could visit the other side of our family. My father never joined us on these adventures. His absence was an unspoken blessing for which we were thankful. As sad as this was, each of us discovered a certain measure of peace by escaping his presence, even if it was only for a short while.

Rosie was a true hostess in the highest sense of the word. Bing equally enjoyed conversation. Together, they loved to entertain visitors in their home. Unlike my mother, Rosie kept connected to her extended family as well as Bing's side. They also had quite a network of friends who popped in during our visits. Rosie was always quick to offer a cold drink or a snack. We looked forward to this routine, for we were unaccustomed to these simple pleasures. I can only assume that my mother wished her marriage had the same kind of stability that her sister enjoyed. We always had good times at Rosie's, and through the years her family was loved by each of us.

I always envied Steven as an only child, not to mention an only child of such great parents! He was a few years younger than me, but our age difference never prevented us from spending countless hours playing together. Like me, Steven loved to play outdoors. Two of our favorite pastimes were playing baseball and army. Unlike me, he had some very cool toys. One toy I especially recall was Fort Apache. The toy came in a square plastic carrying case that when opened up folded out into a splendid replica of Fort Apache. The fort came complete with a regiment of cavalry, foot soldiers, and a band of wild Indians on the warpath. Square walls with painted-on wooden posts were highlighted by a swinging gate and four lookout towers. It was a magnificent toy! Steven always seemed disinterested in playing with Fort Apache. I couldn't figure out why. I can remember having to always talk him in to playing with it each time I visited. I'm sure to him after playing with it a thousand times or so it was just another toy, but to me, it was the greatest toy ever. Like the good kid he was he eventually gave in to my begging. I only made it up to his house about once a month, so I had to make sure I got my Fort Apache fix. I would have given anything for that toy!

Rosie and her family were more than just a welcome escape from our father. Growing up they were practically the sole representation on my mom's side of the family. We treasured their company and I'm sure it was easy for them to conclude that things weren't quite right for us, but just like everyone else, not even they could have known the full extent of what was happening behind closed doors.

Five Inseparable Children

My mother often mentioned how people commented on the exceptionally close bond that existed between her children. I never really gave it much thought until later in life when I realized not all siblings experience the unique bond we shared. We were truly knitted from one fabric—a tapestry of love if you will—that remained intact throughout the duration of our childhood. Like Alexandre Dumas's *The Three Musketeers,* it was one for all and all for one. Now this is not to suggest we were immune to sibling rivalry, we did have our moments. But seldom, if ever, did any of our differences get in the way of our unconditional love for each other. There is little doubt the turmoil in our home strengthened this unbreakable bond. Could there ever be a more powerful representation of good coming from bad?

When I think of our home life, I often compare it to a prison camp where my father was the warden and we were the inmates.

Fortunately for us, the warden rarely stayed in for the evening, but when he did, bedtime always came at an early hour. The main reason for this was my father's intolerance for noise, especially the cacophonies generated by five children traipsing around his tiny house.

Once we were in our cells, I mean our beds, strict silence was enforced. Any breach of this rule was dealt with swift and severe punishment. To combat our sleepless fates, we devised a tapping code similar to the ones you'd see in the old war movies. The code itself was meaningless, but it served its purpose by keeping us connected despite our father's oppression. These acts of defiance usually came to a swift end when one of us could no longer contain our giggling. With a hateful tone he barked out threats demanding we knock off the knocking or he would come into our rooms and knock each of us off to make sure he got the guilty party. We never tested the limits of his threats, but the code signified our united resistance against his tyrannical nature.

John

My brother John was born on July 6, 1956. His hair was jet black. He had the typical round face with which most Winter children were known. From an early age he was rebellious, always wanting to do things his way. His strong-willed nature wasn't that different from many other young children, except he had a father who was extremely short of patience. This combination would spell disaster as they soon became pitted against each other. Through this struggle of wills John became the poster child of my father's fury.

I'm sure when John was born the initial reaction was one of pure joy for my parents. After all, as in every family, the birth of the first child is a monumental occurrence that is looked forward to with great anticipation and excitement. John's arrival was no exception, but as John grew, things slowly evolved from good to bad to worse.

I can still remember hearing horror stories of how John went to school covered with bruises all over his little body from the constant beatings he received from his father. Fortunately for my father, but not for John, this was well before the days when the division of family services promptly showed up to investigate even the slightest of bruises on a child. My mother protested in vain over my father's abuse of his son, but her words fell on deaf ears. Having children myself, it's inconceivable for me to imagine how any parent could tolerate such treatment of a child. In her defense, whenever she defied him, he threatened her with the same fate. This by no means excuses her lack of action. Fear simply won out over sanity.

John was a tough kid and somehow he weathered through these early storms. The stories my mother told me of the beatings John endured from my father terrified me. I was a passive kid to begin with, but when I heard these stories I dared not give even the slightest measure of resistance to any of my father's commands. I wasn't a brain surgeon, but fear can make you intelligent. I did the only thing I could think of. I adopted a low-profile strategy hoping to avoid the same fate as my brother. My plan was by no means flawless, but I'm certain it saved me from a number of beatings.

As time went on, our tiny house became filled with children. John remained locked in mortal combat with my father, except now there were more targets to unleash his rage upon. With five of us running around it diverted some of his wrath away from John, but clearly he bore the brunt of my father's anger.

By the time the five of us were in school, things only got worse. The dinner table soon became the epicenter for many tense moments. The reason for this was that dinner time was one of the few instances during our childhood where we came together as a family. Our father typically arrived home from work around four fifteen in the afternoon. Each of us knew we were to be at the dinner table in our assigned seats at precisely four thirty. When we sat down to eat, my dad was already situated at the head of the table ceremoniously reading his newspaper while he waited for my mother to serve his dinner. The policy was speak only when spoken to. Therefore, we remained silent until our meal was served.

My mother never sat with us while the meal was taking place. Instead, she stood by in silent vigilance, ensuring the needs of her king were met. The meal approval by his majesty was of the utmost importance. This is no exaggeration. On more than one occasion I can recall him hurling his plate of food back at her in disgust. After witnessing this on more than one occasion, we kept our guard up by making sure his first swallow stayed down. This was the signal that it was safe for us to begin eating our meal.

The tension at the dinner table was usually so thick you could cut it with a knife. Periodically he would peer over his newspaper, shooting us a stern glare that without even saying a word meant our plates had better be cleaned before we ever thought of being dismissed from the table. He would then remind us of how fortunate we were to have such an abundant selection of homegrown vegetables that starving children in underprivileged nations would have gladly given their right arm for.

One activity that routinely took place at the dinner table was the review of the household budget. Like clockwork, partway through the meal he would demand that my mother pull out the checkbook to review any financial transactions that occurred while he was away at work. A deafening silence descended over the room as my mother reported each deduction line by line. Many heated arguments ensued. He would stare at her with a menacing eye that sent terror through our ranks. Even minute expenditures were challenged with the utmost ferocity. I'm sure this was part threat and part scare tactic to remind her of what the consequences would be should she ever think of indulging in any unauthorized spending. Heaven forbid that the beer fund should be depleted even in the least measure. We learned from an early age there's never any money in a family with an alcoholic.

As this ugly process played out, we remained focused with the task at hand, cleaning our plates. The only problem was that doing so usually required eating at least four or five different kinds of, well, as my father put it, "heavenly treasures" from his garden. Now if you were an adult, this would have been a delicacy, but for kids this was particularly tough to swallow every night of the week. I'm not just talking about the basic vegetables like corn, peas, and beans that were featured on the majority of dinner tables across the land. Our meals consisted of a smorgasbord of vegetables that included artichokes, rutabagas, okra, eggplant, zucchini, turnips, parsnips, and many other vegetables that few kids could pronounce, let alone have a willingness to eat. I hate to think of how many of those "heavenly treasures" we swallowed whole with our milk each night.

On one occasion, in an incredible act of defiance, my brother attempted to outfox my father by sneaking his vegetables into the pockets of his blue jeans. One by one we nervously watched him remove the unwanted greens from his plate right under the ever-watchful eye of my father. When he had completed the deed, he proudly displayed his clean plate for my father to see. He then politely requested to be dismissed from the dinner table. After close inspection of his plate, my father permitted him to leave the table. We were stunned. It seemed he had pulled off the impossible.

After placing his plate in the sink, John made a beeline for the bathroom door, where he quickly deposited his unwanted veggies into the toilet. Moments later we heard the ceremonial flush and then saw John emerge triumphantly from the bathroom with a bold smirk of success written all over his face. Unfortunately for John, my father arose from the table with an urge to purge. In a disastrous turn of events, some of the evidence from his victory flush resurfaced and was now floating on top of the toilet water. It took my father only a matter of seconds before he realized he had been bamboozled. The discovery of John's crime predictably resulted in my father going ballistic. We watched in horror as John took an unforgettable beating. I'm not sure which was worse, the physical pain John received or the mental pain we endured by having to stand by helplessly listening to his screams.

John would face many more beatings that far exceeded anything the rest of us would bear. For him, early childhood would forever be a dark chapter in his life. My mother was the only defense standing between John and our father. However, as mentioned before, she knew if she intervened she faced the same fate as him. She truly felt guilty for not standing up to my father. She carried that guilt with her until the day she died. This vicious cycle of physical abuse went unbroken for the first ten years of John's life until his deliverance finally came.

Safety at Last

It was a warm summer afternoon on the day the carnage took place in our front yard. There they were, father and son locked in mortal combat, only to be subdued by the one force that neither of them dared to defy, Grandma. When my grandmother arrived on the scene, it was like the shield of God had been placed directly in front of my brother. She declared once and for all that she was taking John from him. After a few more fiery exchanges, he capitulated. That day and for the remainder of his childhood, John became a permanent resident in my grandparents' home.

I watched in awe as she suppressed my father with mere words. The rest of my siblings were looking on too, completely enthralled by my grandmother's ability to rescue her grandson from the sinister clutches of our father. I was baffled by my grandmother's fearless resolve. Her character left an indelible mark on each of us that day. She made me realize that no matter how big the bully, you must never be afraid to stand up for what you know is right.

Later on she told each of us that God watched our every move. It's unacceptable to stand by silently watching while others suffer. She believed without any reservations that whenever confronted with an obvious evil, one must fight the good fight. Her actions were powered by her awareness of God. She was a complete believer who clearly understood the repercussions of one's actions or the lack of. She believed it was better to face the fears of this world than to answer God in the next. This belief not only guided her actions, it eliminated any concerns for personal consequence.

My sisters and I were relieved to know that John was finally saved from the tyrant who had beaten him so frequently during his childhood. The rest of us were thinking, "Can we come too?" But we knew that our grandparents couldn't rescue all of us. Surely John needed their help more than any of us.

Even more astounding was the fact my mother remained speechless during the entire confrontation. I often wondered what was going through her head when my grandmother removed her firstborn child from our home. But then again, why resist it? My mother had to have gained some measure of contentment knowing at least her son was now safe and in a far better place.

After John moved in with my grandparents, things improved almost instantaneously for him. His clothing was the first thing I noticed. He was completely refurbished from head to toe in striking new clothes. This new look bolstered his confidence that was accompanied by a newfound swagger. There was little doubt he had undergone a complete transformation. His metamorphosis was no doubt a direct result of being removed from his father's domain. To be more precise, it was an infusion of godly influence from our grandparents that accounted for his startling change. They deserved all the credit.

I think my grandmother sensed the lopsided disparity between John's new look and my pathetic look. As a mercy offering, she started sending a continuous flow of hand-me-down clothes. However, these clothes were not John's. They had belonged to her sons from years ago. Since she had mostly boys, I became the sole benefactor. At the time, I thought I had hit the mother lode of "snazzy" garments. The sheer quantity of items was staggering. I spread out the cache of clothes on my bed. There were stripes and plaids arrayed in an endless assortment of colors. Needless to say, I wasn't completely sure of what I had, but I felt anything had to be an upgrade over the worn-out clothes I'd been wearing.

I didn't know where to start, so I just began putting on everything. My biggest problem was that none of these clothes fit me. Most of the slacks were a couple of inches too short, but I reasoned I could compensate by wearing them a little lower on my hips. The shirts fit opposite of the pants, appearing huge and baggy over my slender frame. Worse yet, I had zero fashion sense. Nonetheless, I was determined to make improvements. I brushed off these anomalies as a risk worth taking.

After putting together a few arrangements, I was ready to try out my new look. Surprisingly, my mother didn't offer as much as a hint of criticism when I strutted past her in my flashy new look the next morning. I wasn't sure if she didn't have the heart to tell me how absurd I looked or if years of being deprived of clothing herself had left her as clueless of fashion sense as me. Regardless of either reason, I took off for school misfit and mismatched.

Once I entered through the main doors of my school, it didn't take long for me to realize I had made a gross miscalculation when it came to flaunting my new look. Almost instantaneously a volley of insults flew my way. One kid called me Liberace, while other less clever hecklers settled on "circus freak." It soon became apparent I had made myself a centerpiece for ridicule. After a rough day at school, I discarded the passé wardrobe for the rags I had been accustomed to wearing. Returning to my old look was equally demoralizing, but at least it quelled the insults.

Brothers for Life

The following Christmas brought about another infamous memory. Each year a tradition took place where our family went next door on Christmas Eve to celebrate the holidays with our grandparents. My father never attended these family get-togethers. He instead opted for the more soothing environment of the tavern. My sisters would generate a ton of excitement as Christmas Eve drew near. For they knew the gifts we received from our grandparents were vastly different from the ones we'd find underneath our tree on Christmas Day. By this I mean the gifts we typically received from our parents were things we needed rather than wanted.

When that long-anticipated night finally arrived, we made our way over to our grandparents' house to partake in that splendid ritual. After sharing in some eggnog, Grandma would ceremoniously rise from her easy chair to announce the time had come to open gifts. The children would go into a controlled frenzy as they anxiously waited to hear their name called out.

Eydie and Sara were first. They tore into their presents like a couple of wild mongooses. Inside their elegantly packaged presents were two Raggedy Ann dolls complete with accessories. The girls gave their stamp of approval by giving bear hug embraces to each of their dolls.

My sister Kerry was next. Her present was too large to fit under the tree. The sheer size of the gift caught our attention when we first entered the room. When I saw it, I had hoped it was mine. Once Grandma made it clear the gift was Kerry's, everyone let out a few oohs and ahs. Unlike my younger sisters, she exhibited great restraint as she slowly removed the wrapping paper that covered the box. When she opened it, she found a multitude of smaller presents inside; each one was wrapped separately. Grandma instructed her to open them in the order that they were numbered. Kerry followed her instructions to the T. The first ones were gag gifts such as a worn-out shoe and a garment with a big hole in it. This brought laughter from those of us on the sidelines. She continued to open the remaining gifts in the big box. By now my brother and I were getting pretty antsy waiting for our turn. She finally got to the end of her packages. Despite a few more gag gifts, she was piling up some nice things as well. Among these were winter clothing, perfume, and even a little money. My brother and I remained in suspense until she finally opened the last package. Inside of it was a beautiful bracelet she proudly displayed for everyone to see, but not before she had tried it on first. It was finally our turn. I was sure my brother and I would explode if we didn't get our gifts soon.

Curiously enough, there weren't any presents for either of us under the tree. Then, my grandmother stood up again and announced that our gifts were in the small shed attached to their house. The shed could be easily accessed through the kitchen. In that moment, I was sitting closer to the door than John. Being well familiar with the path, I bolted off ahead of my brother to see what awaited us.

Upon opening the door, my eyes locked on to a sparkling, brand-new, bright orange bike with black racing stripes that lined the fenders. I jumped for joy, believing this incredible piece of machinery was intended for me. For a few glorious seconds I basked in this joyous moment until it was shattered by the stern voice of my grandmother shouting out from behind me, "That's not your bike, Jim! That's Johnny's bike! Your bike is over there!" I refocused my eyes across the room. There, sitting in the corner, sat an old, rickety, worn-out jalopy of a bike that had been crudely repainted. I instantly recognized it as the old bike my brother had been riding for years. I slumped over, devastated by the sudden turn of events. I looked over and saw my brother gloating over his new bike as a chorus of cheers erupted from the rest of the family. I did my best to regain my composure.

It would be wrong of me to say I was completely unappreciative of the bike. It turned out to be the only bike I ever owned as a kid. It was certainly better than no bike at all. Stoically I thanked them, but deep down it hurt. I felt slighted because my brother and sisters had received new gifts while all I got was an old hand-me-down. It was moments like these that began to reveal an all too familiar pattern as to where I stood in my grandmother's eyes. Something was definitely wrong, but I was at a complete loss as to what I had done to deserve her resentment.

I wasn't the only one who had taken notice of my grandmother's dislike for me. It soon became common knowledge even to extended family members. Theories developed, but the true nature of her resentment for me would remain a mystery during my childhood and beyond.

One day, I overheard my father and grandmother arguing over my father's treatment of his firstborn son. My father was attempting to justify his actions by suggesting that John, plain and simple, was a bad kid. He chose me to support his theory by pointing out that I demonstrated the qualities of an obedient son. I was definitely obedient, but it was fear that drove that obedience, not respect. As mentioned earlier, I was submissive for the sole purpose of avoiding my father's wrath. As I listened, I literally felt like I was caught in the crossfire, and at the time, I thought maybe this clash between my father and his mother was the reason for her contempt for me. By effectively pitting me against my brother, my father had sowed the seeds of resentment into my grandmother's psyche. I believed from these seeds, a taproot of dislike grew, rapidly entangling her mind, forever refusing to relinquish its grip over her. Although this episode further distanced my grandmother from me, there was still much more to the story. She had shunned me from a very early age, well before this incident ever took place. It would, however, take many years before I would learn the whole truth.

Despite her resentment of me, I still admired my grandmother for giving John a new lease on life. She loved him as if he were her own son. She did a tremendous job of helping him get past the physical and mental scars he had suffered under my father's roof. During my childhood, I never gave up on the hope that she could see the good in me as well.

Despite being torn from each other, John and I had already formed a strong bond well before he was taken from our home.

One defining connection we shared was our love for the game of baseball and the Chicago Cubs. We grew up in the sixties with the likes of Billy Williams, Ernie Banks, and Ron Santo. These "real" heroes were forever etched into our young, impressionable minds. Believe it or not, it was actually our father who initiated this love affair. A few years earlier he had taken us into Chicago on the train to see a Cubs game. It was truly the biggest thrill of our otherwise deprived childhood. After attending the big league game, we became inspired to construct our own *Field of Dreams* in the form of a wiffle ball field in our back yard. Baseball had become our biggest passion, and it also brought us together as brothers.

When John entered high school, a gap developed in our relationship. The coming of age brought with it a change in pursuits. He was in the high school jazz band, participated in speech club, and played on the high school football team. As the younger brother, I remained in his shadow, admiring his involvement with these newfound endeavors.

There were also other interests, such as the "fight club." During the early seventies fighting was the *in* thing, especially at the high school level. It was a time when being tough was more important than being smart. My brother was well aware of the fight club. His network of contacts kept him informed whenever a big fight was taking place. On more than one occasion I tagged along to experience the spectacle. The guys doing the fighting were older and bigger than me. I was still just a scrawny preteen at the time, and I have to be honest, I was pretty much the coward. Whenever we attended these fights, I kept close to the protection of my brother. I was practically his shadow. In almost every fight there was blood flow. Just the thought of being in their shoes terrified me, for I had already witnessed more than my fill of senseless violence at home. Still, there was a certain alluring element to the fight club that aroused even my curiosity. During those days it was like a right of passage. John held a similar fascination with the "fight club" as well, but he, too, seemed content being a spectator rather than a participant.

Within a year the fight club fizzled out, but it did pave the way for a different aspect of the sport, organized boxing. To my complete surprise, John began training for a fight. I had never seen my brother in a fight before, especially in such a structured setting. His opponent was none other than Tommy Sullivan, who, at two years his junior, was a formidable adversary. Despite the age disparity, Tommy was a tough kid who feared no one. I knew he would give John all he could handle.

Just like a professional fight, there was a ton of hype taking place before the main event. The publicity intensified when the two unheralded fighters were paraded up and down Main Street by their respective trainers. It was almost impossible not to notice them strutting around town shirtless while shadow boxing with taped wrists. It wasn't long before the two fighters had captured the hearts and minds of the citizens of Hanover.

On the day of the fight, a big crowd gathered for the main event. The location for the fight was in Johnny and Jimmy Cottral's backyard. It was a hot, sunny day when the two fighters entered the ring. Each was determined to leave his mark on boxing history. From the sound of the bell, both fighters came out punching and didn't let up. Tommy threw a barrage of jabs, roundhouses, and uppercuts while John answered with a similar combination of punches. It's not easy being a spectator when it's your brother out there absorbing the blows. Each time one of Tommy's punches landed directly on John, I could almost feel it myself. I watched in agony as round after round the two combatants battered each other senselessly. When the fight finally reached the latter rounds, it was evident the gladiators had begun to tire. At this point the fight appeared to be in slow motion. It reminded me of the *Rocky* films where each time a punch connected you could see the sweat spraying off the fighter's head. Finally, I saw the ref throw his hands up in the air, signaling an end to the fight. Too worn out to throw any more punches, Tommy forfeited the match. Both fighters had endured a barrage of blows, but in the end John's stamina proved to be too much for Tommy.

When John was announced the winner, he threw his fists into the air to signal victory. He was proud to have beaten such a worthy opponent. There was really no loser in this fight; each participant displayed courage, tenacity, and sportsmanship—all signs of true winners.

Whenever I think of the fight, I've often wondered how much this experience prepared John for what would eventually become his biggest battle, his struggle against cancer. Just like the fight, he kept swinging to the very end.

John and Debbie

By the time I entered high school, John had graduated. Shortly after his graduation, he joined the army seeking a career in medicine. He would return off and on, and the close relationship we shared as youths began to rekindle. After serving the first two years of his enlistment, he met his future wife, Debbie. They met while they were stationed together at Fitzsimmons Medical Base near Denver, Colorado. They married shortly thereafter. By the time I was seventeen, I had saved enough money to purchase a bus ticket to visit them at Fort Dix, New Jersey, where he happened to be stationed at the time. Up to that point, it was by far the biggest adventure of my life.

I boarded my Greyhound bus from the station in Savanna, Illinois. A little less than a thousand miles later, I was greeted by my brother and his newlywed wife in Philadelphia, Pennsylvania. This was the first time the three of us spent time together. Since Debbie had already been honorably discharged from the service, it gave her and me time to get to know each other while John did his duty during the day.

At the time of my visit it was clear John and Debbie had grown tired of the army. I, on the other hand, being unaccustomed to military life, found it quite exhilarating to be on a military base. As a child I had spent countless hours playing army with my friends. I was intrigued by military life and I had often considered joining the service myself. Honor, duty, and the uniform were just a few of the reasons I found it compelling.

Fort Dix was primarily a boot camp and therefore home to hundreds of raw recruits. I was sucked in like a vacuum as I watched the greenhorns performing their drills. John was in his third year of service, and by that time he had risen to the rank of sergeant. He was a medical specialist, so he had little to do with the recruits. When we took a tour of the installation, I got a charge out of watching the regulars salute him every time he came into contact with one of them. Many of those young soldiers didn't look much older than me. I couldn't help but entertain the thought of someday joining their ranks. However, this notion was quickly dismissed when we came across a hulking drill sergeant who was screaming at the top of his lungs right in the face of a scrawny recruit that was maybe a third of his size. I immediately had a flashback to one of my father's tyrannical outbursts. I quickly concluded I had already served enough time under one military regime. I had no interest in doing it again. No, the army was definitely not for me.

My stay lasted two weeks. It was a non-stop ride that included day trips to Washington, D.C., Baltimore, and Philadelphia. In Philadelphia, John took me to the place where Rocky Balboa had made his legendary jog that culminated with him climbing the steps to the Philadelphia Museum of Art and raising his arms in victory. Gasping for air, I did my best impersonation of the "Italian Stallion" as I fought my way up those famous steps. When I finally reached the top, I couldn't resist raising my arms high above my head in Rocky-like fashion. It felt good!

Later on that day we went to see the Liberty Bell and then topped it off by attending a major league baseball game under the lights. The game we went to was actually a doubleheader between the Philadelphia Phillies and the Montreal Expos. The only previous major league baseball games I had attended were at Wrigley Field, back when the Cubs played only day games, so seeing a couple of games under the lights was truly a special treat.

Our seats were in the outfield upper deck. I can still remember thinking how cavernous Veterans Stadium appeared. We stayed for the entire doubleheader. It was eighteen innings of pure bliss. However, shortly after the second game began, a rain delay ensued. It appeared our fun had been brought to a screeching halt. Shielded by the overhang of the stadium roof, we remained in our seats as we watched the grounds crew pull out the infield tarp. Slightly disappointed, we sat back and waited for the rain to stop.

A few minutes after the tarp had been placed down, a fan made his way on to the field. We watched with interest as he attempted to elude several security guards who were hot on his trail. When the security guards started to close in on him, he unexpectedly belly flopped onto the tarp, sliding endlessly head first as if he were a base stealer making a desperate lunge for the bag. Meanwhile, the guards who were after him kept slipping and falling, which only added to the melee. It was funnier than an Abbott and Costello routine. Their ineptness encouraged more fans to join in on the fun. Before long, hundreds of fans started pouring onto the field to take a turn at belly flopping. By now John and I were laughing hysterically. During these moments of uncontrollable laughter, a reconnection took place in our brotherly relationship. As our eyes met, I could sense our past and present were being fastened together. No longer could time or distance sever our brotherly love. We were forever conjoined as brothers and best friends.

When my trip finally came to an end, it thoroughly pained me to leave. I was having such a good time I didn't want it to end. John and Debbie were sad to see me go too, but the trip had revitalized my friendship with John and created a new friendship with Debbie. We knew the next time our paths crossed it would be better than before.

After his discharge, John attended Penn State University, got his degree, fathered a child, and eventually moved back home where he found a job as a physician's assistant in nearby Dubuque, Iowa. I was now in my early twenties. I was ecstatic when I learned my brother was returning home, but to my astonishment, John and Debbie had grown apart from each other. Before long a divorce followed. At the time, his daughter, Sarah, was just a small child, and the prospect of losing both of them tore him apart. I was now living in central Illinois. When they separated, I started making trips back and forth to Dubuque to lend him some emotional support.

Within a year of my brother's divorce, I lost my job and, after much urging from John, I moved to Dubuque. We picked up right where we left off at Fort Dix and the fun never seemed to stop. We started making trips into Chicago to see an occasional Cubs game. We hadn't been to a game at Wrigley since we were kids, so returning there was like visiting an old friend. Strangely enough, it seemed that every time we planned to go see a Cubs game, the threat of rain would attempt to spoil the occasion. Since Chicago was a good four hours away, I had my apprehensions about driving that far for nothing. John, however, being ever the optimist, would look up at the sky and say, "You never know what it's doing at the ballpark." That phrase somehow always convinced me it was a risk well worth taking. Whenever we drove into Chicago we always took "the truck" for these adventures. Once we got on the road, the skies would inevitably clear, and by the time we reached the ballpark we were basking in beautiful sunshine. I couldn't begin to tell you how often we repeated this scenario, and not once did we get rained out.

Kerry

My sister Kerry was born on July 12, 1957, just a little over a year from the day of John's birth. She was the oldest of my three sisters. She, like me, resembled my mother's side of the family. When my brother moved next door to live with my grandparents, she assumed the role of the firstborn child. Kerry and I were four years apart, but despite the age gap, we shared a close relationship in part because I was now the only boy left at home. For all intents and purposes, I had assumed the role of big brother.

She treated me like an equal by letting me be a part of whatever happened to be going on. I really appreciated this, for it gave my confidence a much-needed boost. Kerry was popular in school and had quite a few friends who spent a good deal of time at our house during the summers when we were growing up. Despite the fact that she was a girl and her friends were girls, I was intrigued by their knowledge of the latest and greatest trends of the time.

They often played forty-five records of rock bands from the late sixties and early seventies. This was my first exposure to rock and roll music, and I liked it. They were also schooled in the fine arts of tie-dyeing and Frisbee flying. Kerry and her friends were the masters of fun and games. We spent countless hours playing our favorite games, which included ditch, red light/green light, and dodge ball, to name a few.

"Ditch," was a version of hide-and-seek. The game was always played at night with two opposing teams. There were no limits as to how many players you could have on a team. The playing field was our neighborhood that comprised about four street blocks. Home base was usually the front porch of any one of the homes in the neighborhood. Speed and stealth were the two skills that made up a good ditch player. The first team would hide while the second team sought them out. The team that was hiding had to stay together, which made the task of hiding more difficult. The second team represented the pursuers. It was their job to tag as many players of the first team as they could before they returned safely to home base. Once the second team discovered the first team, a frantic chase would ensue. The chaos created by the chase was uproarious. The pitch-dark blackness of night made it almost impossible to tell who was on whose team. With the members of the second team in hot pursuit, the remaining untagged members of the first team made an obvious mad dash for home base. Semblance would only return when the members of the first team reached base safely. They would then count their losses and switch roles with the second team. Since each team usually had at least ten players, a never-ending back and forth exchange of players prevented either team from getting the upper hand. This flaw in the game's design didn't really matter to any of us because the game was so much fun that rarely did anyone seem concerned about winning or losing.

One of the more memorable undertakings we took part in as kids was the annual carnival that Kerry would stage in our backyard. Putting on the carnival was always an exciting time because this was one of the few opportunities we had to make some cash. Kerry was the unquestionable ringmaster. She represented the brains of the operation while my younger sisters and I played the role of the carnies. In order to get the word out, Kerry would order my younger sisters and me to hop on our bikes and spread the news that the "Winter Carnival" was open for business. We'd tear off down backstreet screaming at the top of our lungs, "Come one, come all, to the Winter Carnival, it's the biggest event of the summer!" This promotional strategy to attract the attention of kids worked better than the music on an ice cream truck. When kids heard our announcement, they gathered their pennies and came running.

We had a variety of games for our customers to choose from. These included the ball toss, penny pitch, and the ever-popular baseball card flip. You could also have your fortune told in a makeshift tent we had constructed by draping a blanket over our swing set. You could even attend a freak show for a nickel—if you had the courage. We boasted two, unique, one-of-a-kind attractions: a man-eating dog and a man-eating chicken. These tantalizing attractions always encouraged the kids to spend their money. After the tickets were sold, patrons would take their seat on a blanket in front of a crudely built stage to watch the show. After much fanfare, the curtain was finally raised. There, side by side, sat my sister Eydie and me, one of us eating a piece of chicken and the other eating a hot dog. Some kids laughed and some kids booed, but nobody ever asked for their money back. You can't find entertainment like that anymore. It was a great time to be a kid.

When Kerry got to high school, things began to change. She landed a job at one of the local grocery stores and the money she earned afforded her some rare luxuries such as clothes, shoes, and cosmetics. These simple improvements did wonders for her self-esteem.

Academically, she consistently began making the honor roll and her sports career took off as well. She became a prolific sports star, excelling in both basketball and volleyball. I loved to attend her basketball games. I watched intently as I kept track of her scoring. She was averaging over twenty points a game! I cheered her on with each swish. I'd proudly sit up tall as if to say, "Yep, that's my sister!" She was hands down the best female athlete of her era. She had become an asset not only to her family but also to her school.

During her senior year Kerry fell in love with a guy from Galena, Illinois. After her graduation they were married and had two children, Joshua and Amanda. I now had two nieces and a nephew, each special in their own way. I remember being an usher at Kerry's wedding. It was the first time in my life I had ever worn a tuxedo. Wearing that tux gave me a lot of confidence. I probably would have worn it a couple more days if I didn't have to return it. Seeing her married and out on her own made me realize my day of freedom would soon follow.

Eydie

Eydie was born on November 18, 1958. Eydie was placed in the unenviable middle child spot in our clan. However, as you will learn, nothing could have been further from the truth in the case of my sister Eydie. Her facial features were extraordinary to say the least. She had the unmistakable round face characterized by the Winter side of the family. Her skin was like ivory. It illuminated her bright blue eyes, fiery pink cheeks, and flowing red hair. Her red hair consisted of the most beautiful locks I have ever seen. When I close my eyes, I can still see her shiny, thick, red hair bouncing off her shoulders as she gracefully competed in red light/green light.

In case you've never played, red light/green light is a simple game where the only skills required are fast feet and quick reflexes. The playing field is very basic. Two designated bases reasonably spaced apart from each other are all that's needed. The distance between our house and my grandparents' garage made ideal bases for a game of red light/green light. Our yard separated the two bases and served as the playing field.

Whenever someone came up with the idea to play a game of red light/green light, the first kid to say, "I'm it," got to face the wall of the garage with their eyes closed. The kid who was "it" essentially controlled the game. Once he or she assumed their position, the remaining players took up their places along the wall of our house. Each of them was required to place one of their hands on the wall while they impatiently waited to hear the magical words *green light*. Once the "it" kid yelled "green light," the others could remove their hands from the wall and move toward the other building at whatever speed they desired. However, once the kid who was "it" yelled "red light," he or she could quickly turn around, and if they caught anyone still moving they had to return to base and start over. Anyone not caught moving was allowed to keep their place and continue their quest of becoming the "it" kid.

Many kids took the cautious route by slowly creeping toward the other base to prevent having to start over. Since I was a daredevil, I would leave base in a full gallop while at the same time attempting to anticipate when the "it" kid would call out "red light." This almost always resulted in me having to return to base and start over. Eydie, on the other hand, also used speed, but she possessed an uncanny knack of being able to stop on a dime whenever the words "red light" were called out. Her body would instantly go into a catatonic state with the exception of that flowing red hair. It would still be bouncing through the air while the rest of her body remained frozen like a statue. This is my fondest memory of her and one I will never forget.

Eydie was a happy, funny child who enjoyed life to its fullest. She was the definition of innocence and always did her best to see the good in everyone, including our father. She loved each of her siblings unconditionally. This quality, along with her steadfast unselfishness, rubbed off on each of us like an infectious disease. In time, she became the invisible anchor of our gang by profoundly influencing each of us with her unblemished character and subtle acts of love.

Some of my earliest memories of her involved the two of us before we were ever in school. Our house was situated on the corner of our street. Across from it sat the parsonage of the United Methodist Church. In the Methodist faith, it was common for pastors to move from parish to parish about every three years. The first family who lived there when we were young was the Foxes. They had a daughter who was my age whose name was Debra. Next to Debra's house sat the Jeffers' home. Toni Jeffers was an only child at the time, and like Debra and me, she was the same age as us. Our closeness in age and proximity helped the four of us to become inseparable friends. Seldom did a day go by where one of us wasn't playing at one of the other's houses. The fact that I was the only boy in the quartet mattered not. It actually worked out for my betterment, for I was cast in all of the male parts in our many hours of fantasy role-playing.

Toni was a very beautiful girl inside and out. At the time, I considered her the most beautiful girl in the world, and unbeknownst to her, she was my childhood sweetheart. The four of us played everything from King Arthur to married life. I think I learned more about women in those years than at any other time in my life. It was truly idyllic, but, like most good things, you don't realize how wonderful it is until it's gone. Debra moved away a couple of years later. The three of us were sad to see her go. A few years after that, Toni also moved. Her new residence was only a few blocks away, which doesn't sound far, but for Eydie and me, it seemed like a vast, unreachable distance.

School provided a means for Eydie, Toni, and I to continue the friendship we had formed as small children. As time went on, Toni became even more beautiful. Her popularity soared. I secretly remained infatuated with her, but I lacked the courage to tell her my true feelings. I reasoned she was out of my league. However, my fear of expressing my true feelings didn't stop my admiration for her; it only grew stronger with time. A huge contributing factor to this was her close friendship with Eydie. Most kids distanced themselves from Eydie, but not Toni. She remained true blue through it all.

Before Eydie was eight years old, something terrible was slowly taking a hold of her. She became ill often and the doctor was unsure as to why. At the time, I was only five. I have a cloudy memory of the initial infliction, in that all I can recall is her being frequently sick and bedridden. Since I was just a kid, I had no idea of the seriousness or the implications of her illness. She was eventually diagnosed with juvenile diabetes. As the days came and went, I, like my siblings, became a witness to the daily trials this incurable condition brings with it.

The first indication that her life had dramatically changed came in the form of a syringe. Once in the morning and once at night, she was injected with a dose of insulin to keep her blood sugar levels in check. Unfortunately, in those days regulating insulin levels was about as easy as finding a needle in a haystack. Technology was a far cry from what it is today. This inability to regulate her insulin levels wreaked havoc on her internal system, causing her to suffer through frequent diabetic reactions closely resembling epileptic seizures. Our family was devastated by her plight. Later in life, I would struggle to understand why God had allowed someone as pure as Eydie to endure such a terrible burden.

Incredibly, Eydie never allowed this tragic turn of events to define who she was. She seldom complained of the hand she'd been dealt, but instead, concentrated on being perceived as just a normal kid. She did an unbelievable job of making everyone in the family feel she needed no special treatment. Her approach relieved the family of much consoling, but the obvious concern for her wellbeing remained a constant.

There was a lot more to Eydie's identity than just high moral character. She tirelessly enjoyed helping my mother around the house with chores. She took an especially fond interest in dishwashing, so much so that the rest of us seldom got the chance to do it. In those days owning an automatic dishwasher was a luxury. I'm sure if Eydie had been offered one, she would have refused it. What most of us considered a drudgery she found therapeutic. I recall confronting her on the subject one day. I asked her, "Why do you enjoy washing dirty dishes?" Smiling and with her hands in the soapy water, she pointed out to me how our dual sinks sat directly in front of the kitchen window. She went on to say how the light entering through the window created a thousand reflections on the myriad of bubbles existing within the soapy water. She described to me how each bubble contained a window with a different color. She then said, "Isn't it the most beautiful thing you've ever seen? It relaxes me to look at them when I'm doing the dishes." Her appreciation for the simple things in life awakened my senses to a part of my world that had gone previously unnoticed. She unquestionably broadened my photographic horizons by teaching me how to stop and smell the roses. This is just one example of how her unique insights helped shape me into the person I have become.

One of Eydie's other passions was crocheting. My grandmother taught her the craft at an early age. After mastering it, seldom did a day go by when she was seen without yarn and needle. Her specialty was potholders. She made countless potholders in a variety of colors that rivaled the reflections of the bubbles in her dishwater. I used to poke fun at her by claiming there would never be a need for all of those stupid potholders.

Eydie was without question the favorite grandchild of my grandmother, even more so than John, who ran a very close second. Their love for each other was like a mother-daughter relationship. They spent a ton of time together, never tiring of each other's company. The rest of us felt left out, but we shrugged it off because we, more than anyone, knew of the terrible hand Eydie had been dealt. At the time, we assumed Grandma took pity on Eydie because of her illness. Nothing could have been further from the truth. My grandmother's love for Eydie was not out of pity. They shared a genuine friendship that the rest of us were more than a little envious of. I have little doubt it was Eydie's character that attracted my grandmother to her. Eydie was the only one of us who could have ever measured up to her high standards of morality.

By the time Eydie entered grade school, the side effects from her illness began to take a toll on her physical appearance. Her entire body from head to toe took on a puffy look due to her reliance on medications. Her eyesight was the first thing to go. With each passing year her vision got progressively worse. This deteriorating condition required her to wear coke-bottle glasses. She selected cat-style glasses, which at the time were quite popular, but I always found them to be unbecoming. I kept my opinions to myself. They were of little consequence anyway. She liked them, and I didn't have the heart to tell her otherwise.

One of the sadder aspects brought about by her appearance was the constant, insensitive teasing with which many kids with handicaps have to deal with. She was inundated with a barrage of insults that frequently included the word *retard*. It never ceases to amaze me how those who are blessed with good health can't resist making fun of those who are less fortunate. I'm sure these insensitive comments were hurtful to her, but I can honestly say I don't ever recall her retaliating. Nor did she ever seek solace, and I mean never. Her positive outlook just wouldn't allow it. I'm still astounded even today when I think of how she took all of this in stride, often laughing in the face of adversity. She was by far the most selfless person I have ever known.

As Eydie got older, a host of complications placed her in an ongoing battle for life and death. Each time she dodged one bullet, some other affliction would be hurled at her that ultimately hinged on her ability to overcome it.

When she was seventeen, one of her kidneys began to fail. Unable to survive with just one, it posed the first serious threat to her life. The family was tested for a kidney donor, but none of us qualified as a suitable match. She then went on the infamous kidney donor list in hopes of finding a match. When none was found, the situation became grave. Saving her life would now require a miracle. In the days that followed, her only recourse would be dialysis.

I had never heard of dialysis until I learned that her survival depended on it. It only took one visit to the dialysis center for the process to be forever engrained in my mind. In those days, the machines were huge with a profusion of wires and tubes that appeared to have no ending or beginning. The process took several hours to complete. Just witnessing it tested one's intestinal limits. On more than one occasion I can distinctly recall sitting by helplessly as I watched the dialysis machine slowly drain blood from one of her arteries, purify it, and then return it in the same slow manner that it had been extracted. During the process, Eydie remained slumped over in a chair. Her body color would become pale white, as if all life had been literally sucked out of her. I stayed there through each agonizing minute, wondering how many times she'd be able to endure these torturous treatments. It became abundantly clear to everyone in the family that the machine that was keeping her alive was at the same time slowly killing her.

Over a year went by while Eydie continued to endure the punishing side effects from the artificial kidney. The machine had taken a heavy toll on her. It was now painfully obvious to all of us that her time was running out.

The year was 1976 and the country was celebrating its bicentennial anniversary. It looked for certain that my family would not be taking part in the celebration. We braced ourselves for the ensuing crisis. We all began praying for a miracle. We clung to the hope that God would somehow rescue her. However, her situation looked so hopeless that we began to grieve for her even before she was gone.

Then, when all hope seemed lost, we received news from the hospital at Iowa City that a match had been found for Eydie. A young girl not much older than Eydie had died in a terrible car crash. We were stunned by the news. Eydie was by no means out of the woods, but this macabre event opened up a window for survival. Eydie was rushed to Iowa City where the transplantation was to be performed. Her condition was very weak, so there were no guarantees. She would first have to survive the surgery before knowing whether or not her new kidney was functioning. The doctors informed us ahead of time of how all kidney transplant patients experience some degree of rejection. The body reacts to the new tissue as a foreign invader and instinctively attacks. Many kidney transplants leave patients with a dependency on drugs to fight the rejection. These drugs compromise the immune system increasing the susceptibility of infection. Despite these looming possibilities, we clung tightly to this one shred of hope, thankful we at least had something to hang on to.

I distinctly recall the kidney being flown in via helicopter to the hospital in Iowa City. Eydie's life hung in the balance as her surgeons raced to complete her transplant. The kidney could only survive for so long out of the body, so it became not just a race for her life but also a race against time. Minutes felt like hours as we nervously waited to hear word of the outcome. Finally the news came. Miraculously, she had pulled through the surgery. Even more incredible, the kidney was functioning perfectly. When I heard the good news, I could scarcely believe it. Never in my wildest dreams did I think she would survive.

Against all odds God had delivered her. When my grandparents received the news, I stood in awe as I watched them fall prostrate with their faces in the dirt, giving praise to the Almighty. Seeing them humbled in this way made me realize I had just witnessed a miracle. Eydie had literally been rescued from the clutches of death. From that moment forward, I began to believe in divine intervention. In time, Eydie would fully recover. Amazingly, her new kidney experienced only nominal rejection. We all desperately wanted to thank the family, whose daughter had died in that tragic automobile accident, but they preferred to remain anonymous, so we did the only thing we could. We thanked them through prayer. Truly this was spiritual renewal at its best;—the loss of one life resulting in the saving of another. It was good coming from bad in its purest form.

In 1978, Eydie and I graduated together from high school. Her repeated confrontations with illness resulted in her being held back a grade. This was a blessing to me, for it allowed us to walk down the graduation carpet together as brother and sister. Being by her side was a greater honor than my own graduation. I was so proud of her.

Setbacks continued to plague Eydie as a young adult. When she was in her midtwenties, I recall visiting her at the hospital during one of her more serious bouts. When I entered her room, I immediately noticed a conglomeration of tubes, plugs, and wires connected to just about every part of her body. It didn't take a brain surgeon to know that she was in a great deal of discomfort. Seeing her like this filled my heart with sadness. On the verge of despair, I leaned over to her and said, "Eydie, if there is anything I can do for you, I mean anything, just name it and I will do it." She looked up at me, smiled, and calmly said, "It's okay. I'm just having a bad day." Her courage was only surpassed by the grace in which she faced her struggles. In all the years of my life, before or since, I have never seen such bravery replicated.

Eydie had gone to church her entire life. During her many years of service, she never once stopped believing in Christ. Her ability to cheat death over and over again still amazes me to this day. Some say she lucked out. Others might conclude that for whatever reason, it just wasn't her time. I must admit that I, too, entertained these thoughts, but having witnessed her recoveries firsthand, I discarded such notions. I became completely convinced it was her faith that delivered her time and time again from the jaws of death.

Eydie went on to fight many more battles that included permanent blindness, poor circulation, and deep sores on her legs that refused to heal. It's impossible to find words that precisely pinpoint her unmatched character. My father was never easily impressed. He summed it up best when he described Eydie as a fierce woman. *Fierce* meaning she possessed great determination regardless of the challenge placed before her. She trusted fully in her Maker. Simple and complex at the same time, her only desire was to be alive and to be part of her family. I know it has been said that it's nearly impossible for a human being to be completely resistant to sin. In the Methodist faith, John Wesley referred to this as sanctification. He believed in it because he claimed to have witnessed it twice. I also believe I have witnessed it in my life, in the case of my sister Eydie.

Sara Sue

My third sister, Sara Sue, was the baby of the family. She was born on August 3, 1963. When she was a toddler she reminded me of a porcelain doll. Sara, like John and Eydie, possessed that perfectly round Winter face. Her features were extraordinary. She had large green eyes, rosy cheeks, and naturally curly auburn hair. Just like my sister Eydie, she had a heart of gold and would do anything for anyone whether they were in need or not.

Sara and I bonded at a very young age, partly because we were the youngest, but more so because I felt it was my responsibility to look out for her. I wanted to protect her in the same way my brother had looked out for my older sisters when they were younger.

Before Sara was old enough to go to school, she received a great deal of attention from everyone in the family, including my father. I'm sure this had a lot to do with her being the youngest, but like Eydie, she had a defining innocence about her. For someone who had little to give, she lavished in giving everything she had, especially in terms of her love, time, and loyalty to each of us. Her heart was pure. She wouldn't have harmed a flea. Her beauty was only surpassed by her kindness. My father would often gloat over her cuteness, especially after he had a couple of beers in him. His favorite saying was, "She's as cute as a bug's ear."

During this time, my father was the leader of a band. His band performed regularly at clubs around the county. He often mentioned a plan to make Sara his star attraction. His idea was to put her in a fancy dress and have her dance around in front of the band as they played. She loved the thought of this, but like so many of his promises, it never happened. It did however demonstrate the effect that Sarah's unique beauty had and how even he was moved by it.

Shortly after Sara entered school, lightning struck twice when she too was diagnosed with juvenile diabetes. The only difference this time was that the doctors were looking for it. They discovered her illness much sooner than Eydie's. Her early diagnosis spared her from many of the complications Eydie faced, but nevertheless she still had her share of touch-and-go moments. Like Eydie, most of her problems stemmed from an inability to regulate her blood sugar levels. This caused her to suffer through a score of violent reactions during her growing years. For lack of a better way to describe it, she appeared better off than Eydie, and although there was a nugget of truth to this fact, it also created a false sense of security. The cold hard reality of it was she was saddled with the same incurable, debilitating disease as Eydie.

Sara now shared the same fate as Eydie. They forever became linked by their mutual illness. My mother always referred to them as the "two girls." This phrase stuck and for the rest of their lives they were referred to by all of our family in this way. Sara and Eydie were truly two peas in a pod. My mother's treatment of the "two girls" differed from the rest of us and rightfully so. Her role as caretaker for the girls formed an inseparable bond that could only be described as special. John, Kerry, and I were never jealous of our mother's devotion to her two youngest daughters. We believed it to be a thing of beauty. Their bond represented the core of their defense against diabetes as well as coping with our father's dastardly acts.

Sara possessed many of the same qualities as Eydie. Among these was her constant concern for our mother's happiness. Like Eydie, she felt sorry for her mother, who endured much from our father. Despite having two strikes against them, they placed their own needs second to those of our mother. I believe their experience with suffering lifted their hearts to heights that few of us can experience. Perhaps it was just another example of good coming from bad.

From a financial standpoint there was very little the "two girls" could do to help their mother. However, they more than made up for it with their helping hands. Each of them performed countless chores around the house. They were not just two of my mother's daughters; they were her best friends. They loved spending time with their mom, and their mom loved spending time with them. More importantly, they recognized the violent nature their father possessed and how their mother did her best to absorb the brunt of his punishment. On more than one occasion, the "two girls" stood fearlessly between their mother and father, acting as buffers. They knew my father would not dare raise a hand against them. Whenever possible, they leveraged this advantage to spare her from any further physical abuse.

Despite their many similarities, Sara was not Eydie's clone. She possessed several unique qualities that were truly all her own. The biggest of these differences was her determination to be perceived as normal by the outside world. Sara refused to let her diabetes define who she was. This was never more evident than when it came to her peers at school. Despite the daily trials of her affliction, she seldom was absent from school. She also kept up her grades throughout all of her school years. She continued to have many aspirations that included being active on the dating scene.

She had a contagious personality, so it wasn't much of a challenge for her to hold her own in the popular cliques at school. Over time she became fairly successful at covering up her condition. Unlike Eydie, she gained the acceptance of her peers and they treated her just as she wanted to be treated: no different than anyone else. People still knew of her condition, but they looked upon her differently than they did Eydie. I know she was very proud to have achieved this acceptance, but it was never in a boastful way. She just wanted to fit in like everyone else.

She surprised everyone when she earned a spot on the color guard with the marching band. We all knew she had tried out, but none of us thought she'd actually make the squad. She was extremely proud of that accomplishment. It boosted her confidence, which opened the door to other successes. The biggest of these was catching the attention of several young suitors. She was more than overjoyed when one of them asked her to go with him to their high school prom. Upon seeing these milestones, my admiration grew for her. I began to see her in a different light than Eydie. She had made a believer out of all of us. She had become her own person. Despite these remarkable gains, there was a downside to her increasing independence. A false sense of security soon developed. It lulled her as well as the rest of the family into believing her situation was not nearly as serious as Eydie's.

Sara's high school years were filled with dreams of moving out and moving on with her life. Sadly, those dreams never came to fruition. The dependency created by her diabetes eventually forced her to accept the reality that she would forever be a medical liability. It was the one thing she could never conceal from the rest of the world. Her dreams of freedom ended with her graduation. The steps she had made toward her independence now tormented her, for it had given her a taste of a life that could never be hers. In the years that followed, fighting off depression would become as big an adversary to her as diabetes. She was hopelessly stuck, and she knew it.

The Wiffle Ball Years

Despite the many dark moments that filled my early life, there was one escape. Once I entered into it, whatever problems I happened to be facing soon disappeared. That world was the game of wiffle ball. The minute I stepped onto a wiffle ball field, I was free. Whenever I played the game, life was good. For me, wiffle ball was more than just a game. It was a sanctuary from all of the hardships I endured with my family.

If given the time, I could go on for hours reminiscing about a golden time when a plastic ball and bat ruled the hearts and minds of many young lads. My days playing wiffle ball are the fondest of my childhood memories. Many friendships were forged on the wiffle ball field and have survived the test of time.

I'll try to restrain my obvious passion for this subject by presenting only those moments that will help the reader to appreciate the impact wiffle ball had on me and so many other kids of that day. Many years have passed since those glorious days, but the fond memories still remain. It was a magical time when the innocence of being a kid playing wiffle ball on a day-in and day-out basis was one of the few things that mattered. In those days, wiffle ball was more of a religion than a sport.

Its origins are shrouded in antiquity, but fear not. I can tell you how it all began. My brother John, his friend Stanley Albright (a.k.a. Tojo), and I were the original architects of the field that would become known as "Winter Wonderland." Our love for the game was inspired by the great major league ball players of the day. Among these were the likes of Mickey Mantle, Willy Mays, Hank Aaron, and the incomparable Roberto Clemente.

Long before either John or I ever knew Stan, he had been given the nickname of "Jap." To many of his peers he looked Japanese, thus the nickname. My brother and I viewed this label as an insult, so we opted for his pseudo nickname, which was Tojo. I always liked the name Tojo. I thought it sounded cool. Now you have to remember that in the sixties, the term *politically incorrect* was still nonexistent. World War II was still fresh in the minds of all Americans, and because of this, the Japanese were still referred to as Japs and the Germans were Krauts. Little did I know that Tojo was the man who had ordered the attack on Pearl Harbor. All I can say is that innocence can be many a splendored thing. Together, the three of us turned the simple game of wiffle ball into an infectious tradition that transformed our lazy summers into seasons of glory.

As time went on, the word got out and wiffle ball's popularity began to spread. Kids from all over town started showing up to play wiffle ball at Winter Wonderland. My mother once told me she counted over twenty kids playing wiffle ball in our yard at one time. Winter Wonderland had indeed become a Mecca for wiffle ball. Other parks began to spring up as well, such as "Cottral's Coliseum," which featured a daunting home run fence and an exclusive press box for announcing games. The press box was a screened-in second story porch that extended off the back of the house. It overlooked the entire field of play, and despite its simplicity, it truly gave the feel of an announcer's box in a big league ballpark. Later on, other stadiums appeared. Among the more renowned were "Miller Metropolis" and "Steed Stadium." Although these other parks were popular in their own right, none of them ever surpassed the legendary status of Winter Wonderland.

Johnny Cottral, one of the original "Wiffle Ball Elites," said this was primarily due to my brother John, who had the best wiffle ball in town. This special ball was made possible by none other than my mother. She purchased a certain type of laundry detergent whose contents included a free soft-seamed wiffle ball that was firm in texture yet pliable enough that you could indent it with a gentle squeeze of your hand. Unlike the rock-hard wiffle balls that you could buy at the local five and dime, this ball not only traveled farther off the bat, it enabled a pitcher to throw an array of specialty pitches, such as a curve, sinker, or knuckle ball. Johnny told me that kids would wait around for hours until my brother John unveiled the special ball. Over time, a fraternity of fanatical wiffle ball players would form the nucleus of a group that became better known as "the Wiffle Ball Elites."

The Wiffle Ball Elites represented a core group of kids who seldom missed a day on the field. Their passion, enthusiasm, and dedication for the game were unsurpassed. Many kids stepped up to the plate, but few achieved the special designation of Wiffle Ball Elite. The names of Winter, Albright, Cottral, and a few others will forever be etched on the tablet of wiffle ball lore. Their exploits on the field can only be described as groundbreaking.

These were the names of the guys who played each game as if it were their last. Proof of their dedication to the game became evident by their blatant disregard for bodily injury while in an endless pursuit of the next great play.

The dimensions of Winter Wonderland were extraordinary in and of itself. The park remotely resembled an actual baseball field and was the furthest thing from being geometrically sound. Home to first and first to second were almost exact in length, but second to third was considerably shorter, and third to home was shorter yet. Home to first was by far the most dangerous base path. This was primarily due to the ever-lurking clothesline that crossed the base path just a few feet before the base. Many base runners were stopped dead in their tracks by the dreaded clothesline. Being short had a definite advantage when running to first base. Our clothesline had a distinct feature in that the lines were nearly invisible. If you became absentminded of its presence, it might cost you an extra base hit or, at the very least, rope marks across your neck. Amazingly, no one was ever seriously injured. However, it wasn't uncommon to see the bench of the team who was batting initiate cheers when a ball was hit in the gap, and then, only moments later, hear those same cheers turn to sighs as the hitter was leveled by the invisible neutralizer.

Other nuances of the field included two trees that stood to the left and right of the pitcher's mound. The larger of these two trees was a tall, densely leafed maple. It stood to the left of the pitching mound if you were the pitcher facing home plate. If a ball off a hitter's bat struck the tree, then everyone on the field would shout "interference!" and the at bat would be replayed. That maple tree took a beating year after year from many ferocious line drive shots off kids' bats that brought down leaves by the bunches... and a few branches too. The tree to the right of the pitcher's mound was a smaller oak. This tree took its fair share of abuse as well, but because of its smaller size, it did not receive the special designation of an "interference" tree. Any balls hit off this tree remained in play, so it paid to know your trees.

Behind the pitcher's mound and the two trees stood our house. If a ball was hit over the house and landed in our backyard, it was a ground rule double. If a ball was hit over the roof and onto Monroe Street, it was ruled a home run. All other balls that hit the house were in play. Also, if a ball landed on the roof of the house and bounced back toward the infield, a fielder could catch it off the roof and the batter was ruled out.

The dimensions of the outfield were equally, if not more, disproportional than that of our infield. Right field was especially short with the next-door neighbor's small shed serving as the home run fence. If you could pop one over the shed, it was good for a round tripper. Most of the Elites were right-handed and were well aware of this flaw in our field design. Many of them attempted to hit the ball to the opposite field, but it wasn't easy and often resulted in an easy out for the defense. I was one of the few who effectively exploited the short fence by learning how to bat left-handed. Since it was my home field, I spent hours perfecting my technique, and before long I was among the leaders in home runs. Some guys admired my versatility while others including some of the Elites became infuriated, for they considered these cheap home runs.

The other unique element of right field was Archie Morehead's garden. Archie's garden stretched the length of his yard and ended where the little shed stood. Archie, like most of the old timers of that day, had a passion for gardening. Much like my father, he grew many different vegetables, and, like so many other gardeners of that day, he loved his vegetables more than his children. To the

Elites, Archie's garden was the dark abyss of Winter Wonderland. Wiffle balls that went into the garden seldom came back. To deter hitters from hitting a ball in the direction of the garden, we devised a rule that any ball hit into the garden was an automatic out. I felt this rule made my left-handed hitting even more impressive, for unlike many others, I rarely landed one in the garden. Thanks to my mom, she kept our stockpile of detergent balls in good order. However, as the summer drew on, we nervously watched our supply dwindle. Archie wasn't as sinister as the Elites had painted him out to be. He was actually a very good friend of our family who tolerated a lot from us kids and always extended the utmost kindness, with the sole exception of those instances when we violated his sacred gardening ground. Despite even this, once his harvest was completed, he would routinely return the cache of wiffle balls he had confiscated from his garden during the summer months.

Left field could only be described as cavernous. It stretched past our yard and included much of Garfield Street along with a large tract of McCormicks' yard until eventually ending at the monolithic walls of McCormicks' two-story house. Prior to those years, Helen McCormick had become a widow, and she now lived in the big house by herself. A row of tall bushes lined the entire perimeter of her house, which helped to create our version of Boston's Green Monster with an added dash of Wrigley Field. The only way to hit a home run to left field was to hit a fly ball on top of McCormicks' roof. This difficult feat enticed many hitters, for there was no higher achievement than landing one on top of McCormick's roof. However, the majority of those who tried were often retired by one of many Wiffle Ball Elites who loved to patrol the grassy knolls in McCormicks' yard. This portion of the outfield provided endless opportunities for diving catches and spectacular grabs. There wasn't a day that went by where an Elite didn't dream of a chance to make a leaping grab against the vines while simultaneously crashing into the wall. Never once did Helen complain of the barrage of kids who routinely invaded her yard or, worse yet, the constant bombardment of wiffle balls hitting her house, or the body of an Elite slamming into her house while attempting a sensational catch. The Elites were forever indebted to her.

Center field was far less romantic than the ever-popular left field. Our house created an unnatural barrier for the majority of center field. The playable area consisted mainly of Garfield Street and the small strip of my yard that ran parallel to this street. The center fielder also had to be on constant alert for any cars or trucks turning onto Garfield Street from either Main or Monroe Streets. Typically, if one was spotted, they would shout out "car!" and all action ceased. Play was not resumed until the vehicle had passed. Many tense moments were prolonged by these untimely intrusions.

Hitting a home run to center was a feat in itself that often lead to controversy. The reason for this is that it required the batter to hit a ball in the air over our house, past our front yard, and then land on Monroe Street. Whenever a ball was hit over the house, it soon left our view. Everyone then froze and listened to hear the distinct sound of plastic hitting the street pavement. If we didn't hear the sound, we assumed it had landed in our front yard and the hitter was awarded a ground rule double. This rule spawned numerous heated arguments. Many bench-clearing brawls arose over disputed home runs. Still, the determining factor was based on audio, not visual evidence. If it wasn't heard, you essentially lost the argument.

It was also possible to hit a home run to left center field. This was a daunting task that was second only in difficulty to landing one on top of McCormick's roof. In order to hit one out in left center, the batter had to launch a ball in the air past the telephone pole that marked the home run boundary at the intersection of Garfield and Monroe streets. This was just as far or farther than hitting one on top of McCormick's roof, but it lacked the allure of McCormick's roof so few kids were challenged by the feat.

Indian Ball

One of the more interesting elements of the game was Indian ball. Indian ball was a phrase used to describe a unique aspect within the game of wiffle ball. Essentially, any runner who was not safely on a base could be thrown at by any fielder. If a runner was struck by a throw, they were out. This brought a ton of excitement to the game, especially in terms of base stealing.

If a runner was daring enough, he could attempt to steal a base, with the only repercussion being that he might get plugged with a seventy-five-mile-per-hour wiffle ball at point-blank range. Just like real baseball, a runner was allowed to lead off any base they occupied as long as the pitcher had the ball. Once the pitcher made his delivery to home plate, the runner would have to return to their base unless the hitter put the ball in play. In Indian ball, the runner could attempt a steal at any time, providing the pitcher had the ball. If the runner passed the halfway point to the next base before the pitcher made his delivery, he was awarded a stolen base. Runners tried to catch pitchers napping, but for the most part, pitchers were well aware of runners and kept a close eye on them at all times. Pitchers, however, were also notorious for playing possum with base runners. They would deliberately prolong their delivery to the plate in an attempt to lure the runner into stealing a base. Runners were always more than willing to oblige the challenge. This cat-and-mouse game was played out thousands of times over the course of a summer, and Indian ball almost became as big as the game itself.

Stealing from first to second was usually not advisable, since the disproportionate field gave the pitcher an unfair advantage. However, stealing from second to third was an entirely different story for a couple of reasons. The first being that the pitcher's back was to the runner, which gave the runner the element of surprise. Secondly, the distance from second to third was shorter, making it a natural temptation for runners to try to steal it. The rules did not allow the pitcher to leave the mound during an attempted steal. This put additional pressure on the pitcher, for it required him to keep one eye on the runner and one eye on the batter. If the runner broke, he had to quickly pivot and fire. Quick reactions were a must if he were to have any chance of catching the runner. If the pitcher threw the ball at the runner and missed, the runner was safe. Seldom did a runner advance more than one base because the opposing teams' fielders were constantly alert, backing up the play. If the pitcher struck the runner, then the runner was out. Indian ball's popularity grew so much that anyone who made it to second base was almost certain to attempt stealing third. This fascinating nuance of the game not only created loads of excitement, it revealed the personalities of both pitchers and runners each time the spectacle unfolded.

One pitcher who was especially feared by base runners was the accurate, hard-throwing, Corey Glad. Corey, the son of a Methodist minister, was hotheaded and coldblooded. He had a special talent for picking off would-be base stealers. He reminded me of one of the old gunslingers from the Wild West. Each time he nailed a base runner he would add another notch in his gun belt. Corey took the game extremely seriously, as if each time he took the mound it was the seventh game of the World Series. Corey loved

Indian ball. For him it was a means of punishing any base runners who had the guts to steal against him. After all, stealing was a sin, and it was his God-given birthright to teach these sinners a lesson.

Over time Corey developed a technique of throwing out runners that would become his registered trademark. Just like a quarterback in football, he would extend his non-throwing arm in a rigid straight line to pinpoint his target prior to releasing the ball. At the slightest hint of a base runner attempting to steal, his face would become flushed, his eyes would pop out of their sockets, and a large vein would begin to visibly protrude from his forehead. As if divine intervention played a part in it, his targeting arm came out while he reached back and fired the wiffle ball with merciless pinpoint accuracy.

When the wiffle ball flew out from his fingertips, it was like a lightning bolt shooting down from heaven. He offered no compassion with either velocity or location. The viciousness of his throws was terrifying. Many would-be base stealers paid a hefty price and bore the welts to prove it. Despite the savagery that Indian ball brought to the game, it was accepted by all as fair play, simply due to the sheer excitement it generated.

I always admired Corey for both his passion and dedication to the game. However, some of the Elites were less appreciative of his accomplishments. Johnny Cottral, a legendary Elite, vividly recalled Corey during one of our many discussions about the grand old game. "I never thought too much of him. Maybe because he picked me off so many times, but I'm sure it had a lot more to do with his intentional punishment of base runners." It was true. Corey relished in the moment whenever one of his ferocious Indian balls made contact. I'm sure Corey threw so hard partly as a scare tactic to discourage base stealing, but he always gave you the impression it was personal. His intense facial expressions made you believe it was his job to unleash hell's fury on you. Corey's style had a profound impact on the game within the game. This became apparent when other pitchers who threw the Indian ball sacrificed accuracy for velocity. The result of this was a huge spike in the success rate of base stealers, but it also tested one's limit of fear; you knew if you got hit, it was going to hurt.

Of all of his peculiar anomalies, nothing seemed to irritate the rest of the Elites more than his patented trademark of wearing a glove when he played wiffle ball. During my many years of playing wiffle ball, he was one of only a couple of players who ever wore a glove. None of the Elites ever wore a glove and considered anyone who did to be a sissy. Corey didn't seem to mind the ridicule. He continued to wear his glove with a zealous intensity. It soon became the punctuation mark on his already maligned reputation. He had taken a different path, but he was an Elite.

Johnny went on to say how he admired me greatly because I was one of the few guys who could consistently steal off Corey, or anybody else for that matter. I always thought of myself as a hitter first and foremost, but if you ask any Elite, they'll tell you I am best remembered for my base stealing antics.

It was hard for even me to deny the uncanny ability I possessed when it came to dodging the wicked Indian ball. I seldom took a big lead off the base, but once the pitcher looked away, I'd take off in a split second with a burst of speed. Sensing the pitcher's awareness of my intentions, I would anticipate his throw by instinctively leaping into the air while simultaneously contorting my body in a variety of positions that rivaled the Kama Sutra. I soon became the envy of my fellow Elites watching in awe as I successfully executed one patented move after another. Many Elites tried in vain to copy my elusive gyrations, but not one of them was able to do so with any regular success. My moves were truly an art form in themselves; each one was unique, which made replicating them almost impossible.

There is little doubt I owe my father for my cat-like reflexes, for it was he who equipped me with my instinctual reactions whenever I became confronted with fear. It was without question a byproduct of my years of being exposed to his wrath. Good coming from bad again. The added adrenaline rush I got from watching so many kids getting nailed by blistering Indian balls on various parts of their bodies only furthered my unique ability. It was as if my fear took on an intelligence of its own. It guided my actions and kept me out of harm's way.

One particular game stands out as my greatest game. It was a hot summer day, and Corey Glad was on the mound for the opposing team. It was a seesaw battle, and I had been a thorn in his side the entire day. In an uncharacteristically low-scoring affair, the two teams were tied at three runs apiece. I had played a part in all three of our runs, and it was late in the game with two outs when I stepped into the batter's box. Corey threw me a couple of brush-back pitches before finally leaving one out over the plate. My eyes opened up and I swung hard, driving the ball into the vines of McCormick's house for a ground rule double. Corey was incensed to say the least, but he soon gathered his composure for the inevitable duel of pitcher versus runner.

It wasn't a question of whether or not I would steal. He knew it and I knew it. I could sense his determination being lifted to a new level. I could also feel the butterflies in my stomach as the confrontation drew near. Undaunted, I braced myself for the challenge. I reached down deep for the equalizer. I closed my eyes and envisioned my father coming after me during one of his drunken rages. At that precise moment, I tore off toward third base like a bat out of hell. After running a few steps, I leapt into the air and then split my legs apart while simultaneously twisting my torso in a manner that would have made a contortionist proud. With my peripheral vision I could see Corey's target arm fluttering in confusion as he attempted to zero in on his target. Still juiced up from the adrenaline charge of giving up the double, it was obvious he put a little more mustard on this one, but it whistled past me as I made my descent. I looked over my shoulder and to my surprise I saw the ball skip through the legs of the infielder who was backing up the play, allowing me to run home with the winning run. Corey was furious! He threw his glove to the ground in disgust. I thought for sure the vein in his forehead was going to burst. I felt the rush one experiences when reaching the pinnacle of success. As my teammates cheered, I realized this game would go down in the annals of wiffle ball history as one of the greatest.

Danny's Gang

Not all of the memories forged at Winter Wonderland were of the glorious variety. We had more than our share of ugly moments as well. Like the time when Danny Moldenhauer and his gang rode their bikes into our yard demanding to take on the Elites in what they referred to as a friendly game of wiffle ball. Danny was the toughest kid I had ever seen. The mere mention of his name sent fear into the ranks of the Elites. The funny thing about it was he was actually a short, skinny kid with long, stringy, blond hair who, on the outside, didn't appear very imposing. However, on the inside he was a rebellious, self-declared rogue, who more than made up for his lack of size with a fearless approach to life that could only be described as reckless. Even the parents in the neighborhood were afraid of him.

On that particular day, a game was already in progress when Danny and his marauders appeared out of nowhere on their bikes. There was Danny, unmistakably riding ahead of the pack. With blazing speed he rode his bike right through our yard. The Elites watched in horror as he made his way toward home plate. After a final burst of speed he skidded his tires, tossing up huge chunks of ground into the air. When he hit the dirt of home plate, he did a spin-out on his bike that created an enormous dust cloud. When the dust finally cleared, I could see the silhouette of his body as he customarily threw his bike to the ground with excessive force. In a loud, authoritative voice he shouted, "This game is officially over! We're now going to play you versus us, and we get first bat." You could watch the heads of the Elites drop in unison as we took up our positions on the field. This wasn't the first time we played wiffle ball with Danny and his thugs. The Elites braced themselves for the onslaught.

Danny and his gang were several years older than most of us, and we knew they could crush a wiffle ball. As the first pitch was tossed, a loud crack of the bat sent the ball whistling past several Elite defenders. Hit after hit proceeded until Danny and his gang had racked up twenty-plus runs. At this point we had two outs on them. In what I thought was a gesture of mercy, one of them finally popped out for the third out. Before we could trot in to take our turn at bats, Danny made another proclamation. In the same bold manner that he had started the game he shouted, "Game over! We got to go!" They hopped on their bikes and tore off as quickly as they had arrived. Relieved, one of the Elites said, "I'm sure glad those guys don't like to play the field."

Kerry Clobbers the Elites

One of the more humiliating moments in wiffle ball history (at least in the eyes of my brother) occurred on a sunny day when several of the Winter Wonderland Elites were being mocked by my sister Kerry for holding the wiffle ball bat with two hands. She thought it was silly that grown boys gripped a plastic bat with two hands as if they were sporting major league lumber. In defense of the Elites, my brother John lashed back at her, proclaiming that silly girls could never compete with the Elites. She fired right back by calling us a bunch of sissies and started boasting that she and her girlfriends could whip us batting one-handed. This insult was too much. Backing down from this kind of blatant disregard for the Elites was not an option. John did what any other Elite would have done; he accepted her challenge.

Now John knew he had put his reputation on the line, so he came up with a scheme he was certain would ensure victory. John was extremely confident that neither Kerry nor any of her girlfriends were capable of hitting a ball on top of McCormick's roof, so he proposed a condition. It basically stated the first player on either team to hit one on top of McCormick's roof would automatically win the game. I spoke earlier in this book of Kerry's athleticism, and unbeknownst to John, I had witnessed Kerry belt a few balls on top of McCormick's roof when she and I were having batting practice in the yard. Being a loyal Elite, I warned John of this possibility, but he shrugged off my warning by defiantly saying, "That was practice and this is a real game." Kerry accepted his condition, and shortly thereafter both sides huddled to talk over strategy. John had only one instruction for his fellow Elites. Go for McCormick's roof on every at bat.

One of the Elites, Terry Fritz, whose nickname was Fritter, took pity on the girls, believing the Elites had an unfair advantage since we played fanatically every day. He added, "Besides, boys are just tougher than girls." So, in a gesture of mercy, Fritter offered the girls first bat. Surprisingly, John didn't seem to mind. He was convinced the Elites would punish them for their disrespect.

Everything was set and the game was about to begin. John was our pitcher and Kerry was their first hitter. This was shaping up into a classic confrontation of sibling rivalry. Kerry stepped up to the plate confidently waving the bat with one hand. The Elites had taken up their positions on the field, certain this wouldn't take long. Unfortunately for them, they were right. Kerry dug in as John went into his wind-up. He whizzed the first pitch in, and when the bat hit the ball, a loud crack followed. The Elites watched in horror as the ball soared off Kerry's bat, eventually landing on top of McCormick's roof. Game over. The high and mighty Elites had been done in with one swing by a girl batting one-handed. To the Elites, her blast became known as the "shot heard 'round the world."

Kerry started celebrating by taking her triumphant game-winning home run trot, but before she could complete it, John had grabbed the bat and began chasing her. He appeared as if he were possessed by a demon. I don't think I ever saw my brother that mad. He chased my sister all over the yard until he spotted my grandfather pulling up in his truck. When John saw Grandpa, he took off, leaving Kerry to explain what had happened. When my grandfather got out of his truck, he asked Kerry what was going on. In a frantic voice she said, "John and his Elites challenged us girls to a game of wiffle ball, and then John said whoever was the first to hit a home run on top of McCormick's roof would automatically win the game. John then pitched me the ball and I hit it on top of McCormick's roof and we won the game! He then got mad and started chasing me around the yard, trying to kill me with the bat I hit the home run with!" Slowly, a half smile came over my grandfather's face as he calmly listened to the rest of her story. When she finished he stoically asked her, "Did you hit it one-handed?" She nodded her head yes, and then a big smile came across his face. That answer provided him with all the explanation he needed. After that day, every time Kerry spoke of her triumph over the Elites, John would cringe because he was forced to relive the humiliation of that fateful day.

Passing the Torch

After a few years, the majority of the Elites entered high school and soon traded in their wiffle ball prowess for other pursuits. The band of brothers was no longer. During those years most of the guys who played the game were around my brother's age. I was by far the youngest of the Wiffle Ball Elites. I was simply lucky enough to be the little brother of one of the head architects who had the special ball and the unique field where kids loved to play. The torch was unceremoniously being passed on to me, but it was more like a flashlight with a weak battery as I attempted in vain to shed light onto a mystical field that had suddenly become pitch black.

In the summers that followed, a large void opened up. The disbanding of the Elites left me starving for past glory. I felt the best years of my wiffle ball career were still ahead of me. I found myself desperately wanting to play, but few kids in the neighborhood seemed interested in the game the Elites had made legendary. Undeterred, I hopped on my bike to begin a quest to regenerate interest in the great sport of wiffle ball.

I did find a few kids around my own age interested, but after a short time it was clear they lacked the passion the Elites had come to exemplify. I started to wonder if maybe the era of the Elites had passed. Perhaps it was time to move on. For a while, that seemed to be the truth, but then one day when I was over at Mike Miller's house with a few of his friends, a spark was ignited. Mike and his friends were a few years younger than I but were nonetheless avid baseball fans. I started talking about the glory days of playing wiffle ball with the Elites. As I began to tell the stories, Mike and his friends who included Tim and Brian Callahan, Jeff and David Steed, and Jimmy Cottral (yes, the younger brother of Johnny who had been an original Elite) all stood by mesmerized with the golden memories of yesteryear. Watching the enthusiasm build in this new breed of Elites excited me to no end. I couldn't help but make comparisons to the original Elites. I looked into their eyes, and without one of them saying a word, I could sense the second coming of the Elites was on the horizon.

When I finished telling the stories we immediately began to survey Mike's yard for any viable possibilities of designing a new stadium. We quickly concluded that our only option was an open section of land that stood at the very end of his property. By itself it wasn't big enough for a field, so, in typical wiffle ball fashion, we annexed his neighbor's yard without permission. The neighbor's yard butted right up to Mike's yard with no fence to separate the properties. It was a huge open piece of ground that was ideal for an outfield. The only problem was it had a pronounced uphill slant to it. But just like the other wiffle ballparks that had predated it, this flaw gave it a signature trademark of its own.

Thinking back on it, it's amazing that not one neighbor ever put up even a mild protest whenever we annexed their yard to form a wiffle ball field. In fact, it seemed whenever a bunch of kids were having some good clean fun, people just unassumingly obliged, as if they felt rewarded by having some indirect involvement. This unspoken bond that existed between the kids and neighbors perfectly illustrated what I have come to refer to as the good old days.

All that remained now was to define the boundaries of the park. Once we configured the foul lines and carved out the bases, the field was ready for its inaugural season. A feeling of renewed glory rushed over me with the ceremonial first pitch being thrown out on opening day. The long anticipation of this moment was upon us. We christened the new stadium by naming it Miller Metropolis. Its inception ushered in a new chapter in wiffle ball history and successfully revived the once sleeping giant of a sport.

Slowly kids learned of the big games going on at Miller Metropolis, and soon the crowds began to swell. I couldn't help but notice similarities to the original Elites that even included a throwback player named Tim Callahan whose nickname was Corky. Corky had a chilling resemblance to Indian ball legend Corey Glad. Just like Corey, Corky enjoyed pitching more than hitting. He also played with a glove, furthering his resemblance to Corey, but it was here where the comparisons ended. The dimensions of Miller Metropolis favored the pitcher which made base stealing much less enticing to the runner. This anomaly of Miller Metropolis once and forever sealed the fate of Indian ball. Indian ball had now been reduced to a mere shadow of what it once was. Sadly, that great chapter in wiffle ball lore never revived. However, despite the diminished popularity of Indian ball, a wave of new young stars emerged with a vengeance as each one of them left their own unique mark on the sport.

Corky was hands down the greatest pitcher of his era. He threw what we all referred to as a heavy ball. Each pitch that left his hand had a sinking action to it that made hitting it a very difficult task. When someone did make contact, it felt like the ball weighed more than the bat and often resulted in a harmless ground ball out. Corky's reputation grew and, before long, hitting a home run off the guy became a feat in itself. By now, I was at a point in my career where I was considered a power hitter. Many battles were waged between Corky and me during my hitting days against him. I was fortunate to crack a few long ones off him. I can remember how awestruck some of the junior Elites were when I was able to drive one of his pitches up and out. Without question, hitting a home run off crafty Corky was by far the most satisfying accomplishment for any Elite during this era.

Miller Metropolis by and large remained the rage of wiffle ball for two summers, but as time went on, more and more kids joined the ranks, making it clear we had outgrown the park. For a short time we started playing again at Winter Wonderland, but the old park didn't have the same luster as it had years before. My father had built a green house for his garden that sat right smack dab in the middle of where the path to first base ran. The two trees in our yard had also grown considerably bigger. These once defining peculiarities were now hindrances because they blocked too much of the available hitting area. If wiffle ball was going to thrive, we'd have to come up with a new field, but where?

Before Miller Metropolis's popularity died, two new kids named Jeff and David Steed started showing up for the games. It wasn't long before Jeff and I became good friends. I soon learned that his family had moved in to what used to be the Tyse house. It was a stately home situated on top of a hill across from the Catholic Church. Otto Tyse had a flair for architecture. He had built the place himself, designing each room with its own unique flair. Two enormous pine trees stood undaunted, as if guarding the entrance to his house. A long straight fence covered with grape vines marked the eastern boundary of their property. Beyond the fence was an overgrown field that was owned by the Catholic Church. It contained a parking lot used to supplement the excess of Sunday parishioners.

One day Jeff invited me over to his place. We went upstairs to his room to brainstorm with the sole intention of coming up with a new location to play wiffle ball. While standing in his room, I looked out the big window that faced the open field. The idea hit me like a ton of bricks, but before I could get the thought out of my head, he had already deciphered what I was thinking. I can still remember hearing him say the words, "It's perfect!" With blinding speed we flew down the stairs and headed outside. We immediately began surveying the rough parking lot while at the same time we pondered our options for a new field. Before long we concocted a plan whose fruition was the creation of a beautiful new wiffle ballpark appropriately named Steed Stadium.

The lot itself was flat, but it was laden with dense weeds and brush. It also contained quite a few large rocks that would have to be removed. Jeff came up with the idea of using his dad's lawn mower to clear the brush and weeds. I was in charge of removing the stones while he began to mow. In one afternoon we had transformed a dormant parking lot into a majestic wiffle ball field. In the great tradition of the past, we were once again building a field on property that was not ours.

The next phase was to determine the dimensions for the park. This was quite easy for we already had a vine-covered fence that closely resembled Wrigley Field's elegant home run wall. Unlike the parks we played on in the past, the field itself was perfect in terms of its flatness and spatial design. It also lacked the familiar flaws that plagued its predecessors such as trees, hills, buildings, and streets. When finished, it was the first wiffle ball park to actually resemble a major league stadium.

We wanted to make sure that the distance from home plate to the fence was challenging but still attainable. The playing field was big enough that we could pretty much put home plate wherever we chose. Unable to decide on an exact spot for home plate, we did the only thing we could think of: we had batting practice. Jeff and I launched a few drives toward the fence to find the range, and before long we had our spot. I must admit the rush one got watching a ball sailing over the vine-covered fence was captivating.

We then completed the finishing touches on our new field by marking off the bases. Jeff and I stood back to admire our engineering feat. It was a proud moment. With its vines and spacious lush green outfield, the park took on an uncanny resemblance to Wrigley Field. It was a place where any of the original Elites would have felt honored to play. Unveiling this technological wonder almost brought us to tears. Once the word got out, kids swarmed to the new field. Soon thereafter, lasting memories were forged at Steed Stadium. The ever-present possibility of making a spectacular catch while leaping up against the vines to rob a hitter of a would-be home run had quickly become every kid's dream. I couldn't help but think of Winter Wonderland and the original Wiffle Ball Elites.

Steed Stadium quickly established itself as the premier place to play wiffle ball. As co-architect, I felt a special relationship with this field. My play would back this statement up as I quickly established myself as the top power hitter. Over two seasons I had racked up more home runs than anyone, and, oh, those defensive gems. I had truly returned to wiffle ball heaven. Then one day something snuck up behind me and stared me square in the face. I had been hit by the sudden realization that my wiffle ball days were coming to an end. I was by far the oldest of this new generation of Elites. I was entering my first year in high school, and the time for me to hang up my cleats and retire from the great old game was fast approaching.

I would now take my place alongside the old Elites in that eternal shrine known as the Wiffle Ball Hall of Fame. That's the problem with time. It doesn't wait or even slow down for anything or anyone. Things never stay the same, and the old cliché that all things must come to an end could not have been more truthful. I reluctantly accepted my fate, but I will forever remember those magnificent days spent on the wiffle ball fields of Hanover, Illinois. Many years have passed since those days. Whenever I return home, I still manage to bump into a few of the old Elites and reminisce about the glory days. As we speak of those priceless times I still see a twinkle in their eyes, validating that these were truly the best of times.

On one of my more recent visits to Hanover I caught up with Johnny Cottral. We spoke at great length, reliving those glory days. He suggested we arrange an old timers' game to relive those magical days just one more time. We ran the numbers and concluded that there were still plenty of passionate veterans who would be more than willing to lace up their cleats and take the field one more time. Maybe all things don't have to come to an end; at least, not for a little while longer.

The paternal grandparents, Orma and Sally.

My parents on their wedding day, George and JoAnne.

Five inseparable children – John, Kerry, Eydie, Jim, and Sara.

Two wiffle ball elites, John and Jim.

My son Zach, standing at the left spire of the Big Tree.

My wife Aimee and son Zach standing at the right spire of the Big Tree.

Split view of the two giant spires that comprised the Big Tree.

My son Zach at the right spire

Hanover, Illinois.

My father and his buddies at the Big Tree. My father is standing
far left at the picnic table. This picture represents the only
known photograph of the Big Tree while it was still standing.
Only the far branches on the right spire can be seen.

My Perspective

Early on in my life it appeared that I was destined to be the sickly child of our lot. Before the age of five I had been hospitalized for an appendectomy, a tonsillectomy, and a double hernia. I don't remember much of it, but my parents were convinced I was their token unhealthy child. However, as I have come to learn, things aren't always as they appear on the surface. By the time I started attending school, the illnesses I had been plagued with in my early youth vanished. Rarely has sickness found me since.

Outside of my home life, growing up in Hanover was a good experience. Living next door to my grandparents turned out to be the biggest blessing I ever received from the Almighty, despite failing to recognize it as a child. They represented solid ground in an otherwise shaky world. School was school. I made plenty of friends, with the exception of a few bullies, but every kid has to put up with that at one time or another during their childhood.

Our House

I remained somewhat oblivious to the "unique situations" of my family until I reached my teen years. It was at that time I began to notice a stark contrast between how we lived and how most of our neighbors lived. It was becoming abundantly clear that something wasn't quite right. My father had a decent job all right, but his unquenchable thirst for beer undermined his responsibility of providing a sound home for his family. The older I got the more glaringly apparent the dysfunction became. Even the most basic of necessities, such as shoes and clothing, were being sacrificed for the ever-consuming beer fund.

The tiny two-bedroom house we lived in was completely inadequate for the seven people who attempted to harmoniously coexist within its walls. The house itself was a plain rectangle with drab green siding accentuated by dark green-and-white-striped awnings that rested over each window. The inside of the house contained four rooms and a tiny bathroom. The four rooms were a kitchen, a living room, and two bedrooms. Unlike many of the homes in the neighborhood, household furnishings were practically nonexistent. The kitchen was the one exception to this rule. It had a modern fridge and stove, table, and chairs, and all of the cooking accessories needed, but only because these amenities were considered a necessity by my father. The living room doubled as my parents' bedroom with the only furniture being a television set, an outdated stereo console, and a broken-down rollout bed. From as early as I can remember, my parents never ever replaced any of their furniture, minus the television set that died after ten years of use. On more than one occasion, my grandparents urged my father to build on to the tiny house, but in his predictable stubborn way, my father ignored their advice.

The bedrooms were small, each containing two beds and one dresser that had to be shared not only with siblings but also with parents. My sisters had regular mattress beds, a luxury by our standards. John and I were less fortunate. We slept on army surplus cots that my father had salvaged from the Savanna Army Depot. These cots came with a wafer-thin mattress that sat on naked box springs. The springs were so rusted that the slightest pressure caused the bed to squeak like a startled mouse.

I never realized until much later in life that wealth isn't just exclusively measured through the acquisition of creature comforts. I spent a good portion of my youth feeling cheated by my meager conditions while all the time right underneath my very nose was a veritable gold mine of genuine human love that flowed continuously to me from my grandparents, mother, and siblings. This was a true and lasting richness that nothing or no one could ever take from me. I was engorged with the genuine riches of love, family, and respect, those elusive intangibles that every man strives to attain. I was wealthy beyond my wildest dreams, but I failed to recognize it only after it was gone.

Looking back on my childhood, it's easy to see that the most valuable thing I ever possessed were the times I spent with my family. My prestige was to be called brother, son, and grandson. It's a shame most people don't realize the best moments of their life until after they've past. In my case, I'm certain that my awareness of this incredible profusion of love was obscured by my fixation on the lack of creature comforts within my immediate surroundings. This unmitigated truth is a regret I still carry with me today.

Like most young boys I thought my mother was the most beautiful woman I had ever seen. If possible, she would have been the person I married. She loved her children unconditionally and gave her very best to each of us. She was a ray of sunshine on a dreary day. She was the one constant in our everyday lives that never wavered. She always found a way to make each one of us feel special. Then there was my dad. They say opposites attract. No statement could more perfectly describe the relationship that existed between my mother and father. I'm certain it wasn't always this way. There had to have been tender moments, otherwise there wouldn't have been so many children.

Painful Lessons

I've always been a firm believer in the checks and balances of one's behavior. To me, human accountability is much like physics. For every action made, whether it be positive or negative, there is an equal and opposite reaction. It might not be today and it might not be tomorrow, but at some point the scales will be balanced. In the case of my father, he acted with complete impunity. He was clearly devoid of any understanding of the damaging repercussions that resulted from his actions. To fully appreciate the depths of my father's noxious behavior, I have selected a few snapshots from my childhood that defined what life was like growing up under his roof.

The earliest recollection I have of my father took place during a rare father and son stroll. I was perhaps three or four years old at the time. I can vividly remember trying to keep up with his massive strides. I'm sure I had to take at least four or five steps for every one of his. He didn't seem very concerned about me falling behind; he just kept going. In order to compensate for my short steps, I had to jog to keep up.

By the time we had reached downtown, I was fairly winded. We then headed toward the bridge that crossed the Apple River. It was the first time I had ever walked across a bridge. My fear began to elevate as we approached it. I became even more frightened when I glimpsed the rushing water of the Apple River. I wasn't tall enough to look over the railing, but below it were a series of hollow arches stretching the length of the bridge. I could clearly see the swiftly moving current through the arches. Then, unsuspectingly, my father grabbed me under my arms and lifted me over the side of the bridge. As I dangled there suspended only by his hands, I felt my life flash before me. I feared he might accidentally drop me, and then surely I would drown. As I was forced to hang over the bridge for what seem liked an eternity, he mercilessly threatened, "If I dropped you, you'd be dead!" Finally he pulled me back and only then did my heart return to its chest cavity. This incident marked my initiation into his dark world of psychological warfare. This continual use of fear tactics prevented any of us from ever feeling secure. Our imaginations became our own worst enemies as we remained imprisoned in a state of perpetual fear, never fully knowing the boundaries of his terror.

My first incident of physical abuse occurred shortly after the bridge incident. Although I'm unable to remember exactly what triggered it, I distinctly recall receiving a severe spanking from my father while my mother stood by helplessly watching. It was a traditional spanking in the sense that he was sitting down and I was lying across his lap. The beating persisted until the force of his blows caused me to urinate on him. I can still hear him yelling in disgust to my mother, "He pissed all over me!" My mother pleaded back, "You're hitting him too hard!" Luckily for me the result of my actions brought a swift end to the ordeal. Looking back on it, had I known the effect it created, I would have done it much sooner.

It's truly amazing that none of us turned out to be like him. Fortunately for us, our lives were filled with extremes. While my father represented a darker version of parenting, my mother and grandparents occupied the opposite end of the spectrum. The example they portrayed salvaged our nurturing, which undoubtedly prevented that terrible part of history from repeating itself in each of us.

My father lacked just about every parenting skill known to man. One in particular I found extremely troubling was his inability to take the time to teach his children anything. Seldom were instructions given, even for life's most basic lessons. If he happened to discover some inadequacy that we possessed, he appeared utterly baffled as to how this lack of knowledge could have possibly occurred. The classic example of this took place when I was five years old. It will forever be engrained in my mind. I was playing outside one day when my father noticed my shoes had become untied. In a stern voice he called out for me to tie them immediately. Unable to perform his demand, I reluctantly admitted I didn't know how, a big mistake on my part. He ordered me inside where I was to begin a crash course in the art of shoe tying. He ordered my mother to get him an old shoebox lid from one of our closets that he quickly fashioned into a practice tool by placing two holes in the center of it and threading a shoelace through the holes. Now on the surface, this was actually a good idea, but deep down I knew once the training began, I had one shot and one shot only to get this right. There would be no second chances, and if unsuccessful, all hell was poised to break loose. After we sat down, he looked me straight in the eye and in a nasty tone said, "Now watch!" Without uttering a word, he quickly began to tie a bowknot. Upon completing the task he quickly undid the knot and tossed the shoebox lid at me. Then, in a sinister voice he said, "It's your turn now!"

Trembling with fear, I tried not to think of the consequences if I failed. I took a deep breath in an attempt to collect myself so

I could focus on the job at hand. I did fine until I got to the part where the lace had to pass through the tiny opening that completed the knot. I hesitated for a few seconds as I tried in vain to recall the step that would get me to the promised land. With the pressure mounting, I could feel my concentration beginning to slip. I tried to buy more time by retracing the steps, but it was hopeless. I couldn't remember which finger to use to complete the knot.

Meanwhile, it had become apparent that the miniscule fuse that was connected to my father's temper was just about spent. My fingers were now working frantically out of desperation, but the harder I tried the more it looked as if I had two left thumbs. My feeble attempts only served to exacerbate his already fervent rage. I knew by the increasing volume of his words that the level of his anger was reaching critical mass. I watched in horror as his appearance began to transform before my very eyes. His eyes began to pop out of their sockets. His face became so red that if I pricked it with a pin it would have surely exploded. Spit was flying from his mouth with each barking word. His cork was on the verge of blowing. I glanced over at my mother, hoping somehow she could rescue me from the coming onslaught. The look on her face mirrored my despair, so I did the only thing I could, I braced myself for the fury. As expected, he lunged toward me. Uncertain of his intentions, I instinctively flinched. He grabbed my hand at the palm and squeezed so hard that it forced my fingers to stand at attention. He then shouted, "It's not this finger. It's this one!" He then bit the finger I had failed to employ while attempting to complete the knot. The force of his bite was excruciating. It immediately brought me to tears. Amazingly, he failed to break the skin and draw blood. He then released my finger from his jaws. As I wept, he ordered me to try again. I fought back the tears, for I knew I dared not show weakness. I gathered my senses and worked my way back to the point I had been before. This time, I easily identified the correct finger from the freshly indented teeth marks. I went on to successfully complete the knot. In an eerie, somewhat relaxed voice he said, "Now that wasn't so bad, was it?"

That day I learned something more than just tying my shoes. I discovered how fear could be a tremendous motivator. I myself would never condone such perverse tactics as those used by my father, but I did, however, come to realize, if used in moderation, instilling a little fear can effectively nudge a person in the right direction. I guess you could call it good coming from bad.

Further testament of my father's corruption surfaced one night while I was fast asleep in my bed. In a drunken stupor he barged into my room, waking me from a sound sleep. He ordered me to get dressed. He then told me we were going outside to hunt night crawlers. He informed me he had personally volunteered to supply worms for him and his beer-drinking buddies for the next day's fishing trip. Of course I wasn't invited, but he still needed a butt boy to do his dirty work. John had already moved in with my grandparents, so I represented his lone option.

I was completely clueless when it came to catching night crawlers. To be completely honest, I didn't even know what a night crawler was. Rain had been falling steadily for most of the day, but by late evening it had slowed to a drizzle. Before venturing out into the yard, my father gathered up the necessary tools for the job. He had with him an old coffee can, a flashlight, and of course, a freshly opened can of Hamm's beer.

The ground that night was completely saturated from the incessant rains of the past twenty-four hours. The grass was clearly in need of mowing. The soles of the beat-up pair of tennis shoes I had on were worn smoother than a baby's butt. Factor all this into the tall, wet grass, and you have the makings for some very slippery footing. Still clueless as to what a night crawler was, it didn't take long for me to find out. Once we stepped outside into the pitch black of night, my eyes became drawn to the only available light source: the streaking light coming from the flashlight as my father made his way across the yard. While following behind him I spotted one of the slimy devils I had been shanghaied into hunting. I thought to myself, *"Why me Lord?"*

My father's instructions were to the point. He would be the seeker, and I would be the catcher. Once an earthworm was located, it became my job to get him into the coffee can. Other than their slippery, gooey appearance, it seemed simple enough, so I began to mentally prepare myself for the task at hand.

It didn't take long for my father to eye a huge night crawler fully extended from its hole. Inside I let out a little gasp, but I knew from past experience I dared not show any cowardice. When he targeted his makeshift spotlight on the nematode, I instinctively lunged at the slimy serpent. However, my poor traction coupled with the lightning quickness of the worm easily allowed it to escape my clutches. When my father observed the worm darting safely back into its hole he promptly gave me a well-centered kick in the butt. This was followed up with a chorus of obscenities.

My next attempt wasn't much better. I managed to get a hold of the earthworm this time, but when I tried to extract it from its hole, it broke in half with its entrails spewing out on my hands. This second failed attempt was followed by another direct kick in the butt. He was now fuming over my incompetence. In a disgusted voice he shouted, "That's not how you catch 'em!" (As if I had received a degree from the Institute of Wormology.) He continued, "You pin 'em down, you jack 'em off, and then you pull 'em out!" Rubbing my sore bottom and shaking my head, I wasn't quite sure what that meant, but I knew I had better not miss again.

Unfortunately, the vile varmints continued to get the best of me. With each failed attempt, my already sore bottom received another punishing blow. He kicked me all over the yard that night, but before it was said and done, I had earned my father's praise. At the end of that terrible ordeal he anointed me with the title of Head Master Baiter. My naivety actually enabled me to take pride in this hard-earned title. In one night I had become the best night crawler catcher in the county! Sadly, though, I began to realize the pattern of his perversion. It was becoming quite clear that what I had perceived as parental teachings were nothing more than me being manipulated through fear to fulfill his selfish needs. It soon became clear to me that he had zero interest in teaching me anything.

My True Father

Shortly after this unforgettable event, my grandfather caught wind of my interest in fishing. One day he summoned me over to his garage where he unveiled an old cane pole covered in dust and cobwebs. When I first laid eyes on the relic I thought for sure I'd never catch a single fish with it. But knowing how badly I wanted to fish, I soon realized that beggars can't be choosers so I wholeheartedly accepted his gift. Although it was primitive in comparison to what many of my friends were fishing with, it gave me my first taste of the sport. A few of my friends poked fun at my pole, but I wasn't discouraged in the least. I actually caught quite a few fish with that old pole. More importantly, my friends soon discovered my prowess for night crawler catching. This talent quickly elevated my popularity with my fellow fishermen to celebrity status. Good coming from bad strikes again.

Unbeknownst to me at the time, I was gaining an understanding of what real parenting meant. Clearly I was learning how not to act. My father's examples of parenting were so improper that even to a child it was obviously wrong. Over time I came to despise his perverted and misguided acts of parenting. On the other hand, my grandfather's ways slowly took hold of me, engraving a positive, lasting impression upon me. I slowly began to see the world through his eyes. I began to seek his advice even when minor decisions arose. He became my mentor without me asking or him offering. I discovered all I needed to do was to be around him, for the goodness inside of him poured out freely requiring no coaxing on my part.

Another indelible memory I have were the army surplus haircuts my father issued to my brother and me at the onset of every summer vacation. This was not your ordinary flat top. We're talking haircuts so short you couldn't tell if we were bald or scalped. By the early seventies the short hairstyles had given way to long hair, so each time it came to receiving one of these haircuts, we felt as if we were marching to the executioner's chair. Once the deed was done we silently walked off, utterly dejected with heads hung low. Afterward we knew we'd have to face continual ridicule from just about every kid we came in contact with. Ball caps became standard issue as we did our best to conceal our bald heads.

Just when the humiliation seemed inescapable, my grandfather had a knack of appearing out of nowhere. He was more than keen enough to detect our sunken spirits. He quickly relieved our worries with one of his soothing anecdotes. As soon as we made eye contact with him he shouted out, "Oooohhh the butch haircut! Now that's the haircut to have. You're not flopping that mop around." He'd go on to tell us how professional ballplayers swore by the butch haircut. The more he spoke the more we reevaluated our predicament. We eventually decided that maybe the butch haircut wasn't that bad after all.

Oh, You Damn Fool!

Over time our grandfather became the dad we never had. Some of my fondest memories of him occurred during the hot summer months of the early 1970s. After he had retired from the Savanna Army Depot, he became the sexton of the local cemeteries. Just like every other pursuit in his life, he took it seriously by approaching it with great integrity.

As the sexton, he was responsible for the upkeep of the three large cemeteries that existed within and around the township. Mowing these cemeteries was by far his biggest challenge. Two of these cemeteries were located in town adjacent to each other. They were appropriately named the New and Old cemeteries. The New Cemetery was home to the more recently deceased generations, whereas the Old Cemetery was comprised of graves dating back from the Civil War up to World War I. The third and largest of the cemeteries was Lost Mound. Lost Mound was located about ten miles outside of town. Its isolation along with the fact that no one had been buried there in years added to its namesake. I always thought of it as more of a historical landmark than a cemetery since it contained a number of gravestones that predated the Civil War.

The township provided my grandfather with a red Ford truck. The truck was needed to transport himself, his team, and the mowers he used to and from the cemeteries. The red truck would become a symbolic representation of his presence to our family and the community. Located within the New Cemetery was a large white garage. It housed the arsenal of mowers my grandfather used to cut the large tracts of grass in the cemeteries. This garage was the nerve center of his operations, and his team always began their day at this site.

My brother John, who at the time was living with my grand-parents, had already been mowing for my grandfather for several years. I admired him in this role, hoping one day I could follow in his footsteps. I myself had been mowing yards in the neighborhood for the past couple of summers. My grandfather let me use one of his personal mowers as a means of earning a little money. He went a step further by splitting the cost of the gas with me. In return, I mowed his yard and continued to work hard to hone my craft, hop-ing he'd notice my handiwork and someday offer me a job working for him at the cemeteries. It never once dawned on me that the entire time he had been training me for the very job I was seeking.

Then, one day, completely out of the blue, he came over to my house and asked me if I wanted a job cutting grass for him. My mother knew this had been a long-awaited moment for me, so when I looked at her for approval, she simply looked back and said, "Aren't you going to answer your grandfather?" Without the least bit of hesitation I said, "Yes!" He told me to be ready first thing in the morning. I was so excited, for on many occasions I had watched my grandfather and brother ride off together to mower heaven, hoping that some day I, too, would have a chance to leave my mark on this great tradition. I felt honored in the moment and couldn't wait to prove my worth.

Early the next day I arose looking forward with great anticipa-tion to my first day on the job. Raring to go, I watched my grand-father back the big red truck out of his garage and then slowly pull up to the sidewalk that led to my front door. I came running out at full speed. I leaped into the back of his truck where my brother was already sitting.

We made a brief stop to pick up John Mason, who, like my grand-father, was retired from the army depot and employed by the township to assist my grandfather. John Mason got in the front cab with my grandfather, and the four of us were off to the New Cemetery.

When driving through our town I remember being awestruck by the unobstructed view we were enjoying from the back of my grandfather's truck. Despite our close resemblance to the Beverly Hillbillies, there was something unique about the way the world was rushing around us. The sights, sounds, and smells of the morning were ubiquitous. A fine layer of mist had blanketed the grassy yards. A gentle breeze caused the vast number of trees and an array of flowering plants to wave at us as we passed by. Completing this frenzy of life were the bustling cars and hustling villagers going about their business as they started their day. I recall looking over at my brother with his hair blown straight back from the force of the wind. He was wearing a face of unrepressed confidence. He turned to look at me and I could sense the baton being passed from big brother to little brother. I sensed something more that stirred my soul, the unmistakable winds of change. I realized he wasn't going to be there forever, but for now, this was our moment together.

After completing the perfectly straight three-block journey through Main Street, we made the big turn toward the bridge that crossed the Apple River. I took notice of the swiftly moving river that split the north end of town in half. Its appearance was one of peacefulness and beauty, unlike the one I recall dangling over in terror just a decade ago.

After crossing the bridge, we turned left and drove along the road that paralleled the river. Shortly after the town was first settled in 1829, a natural drop in the Apple River provided an ideal location for a dam and mill. I could now hear the deafening sound of the water crashing over the dam. Gazing down at the dam, I became hypnotized by its iridescent appearance which was created by endless waves of spraying water and illuminating sunlight. Looking beyond the rainbow effect, I couldn't help but notice the stark difference between the hydrated vegetation that was clinging to the riverbank and the parched, more envious flora growing behind it. This drier flora was desperately stretching toward the river in a vain attempt to satisfy its craving for moisture. By comparison, the brilliant, lush, green plant life clinging to the riverbank was second only in beauty to the majestic weeping willow trees skirting the river. Their whips were swinging ever so gracefully back and forth, coaxed by a warm breeze that gently made its way through the valley.

The road passed by the Old Cemetery before continuing down the hill and around the bend until you reached the New Cemetery. These two cemeteries were connected by an old, rickety wooden bridge that crossed over a tiny tributary of the Apple River. The bridge became a favorite rest spot whenever I mowed in either of these cemeteries. I enjoyed many lunches among a kingdom of living things that included hummingbirds, butterflies, amphibians, and a flourishing variety of plants all peacefully coexisting within this tiny ecosphere.

When we arrived at the shed in the New Cemetery, my grandfather had us rest two wooden planks on the tailgate of his truck to load the mowers into the truck bed. I always admired the contingent of bright yellow Hawn Eclipse mowers that were lined up like troops ready for battle. There were four in all, including one self-propelled model that was the pride of the mowing fleet. This mower, a technological wonder for the time, was solely used by my grandfather. The other three mowers included two standard models, and a junior model that had my name written all over it. This little mower would mark the initiation of my mowing career at the cemeteries. Later on I would eventually move up to the standard size model.

That particular day we were mowing the oldest of the three cemeteries, Lost Mound. As mentioned prior, not a soul had been buried in Lost Mound for years. It was the first cemetery in the area and was built sometime after Hanover was being settled in the late 1820s. The early lineages of many of the established families of the time were laid to rest within its confines. I was astounded at how many of the names etched on the stones were still legible. Many of the names were represented in the present day by their descendents, who were still living in the township.

The sheer size of this cemetery was staggering. Less than one third of it had been used for plots. A large, flat, grassy area that accounted for over half of its size was referred to as the football field because of its obvious resemblance. Not a single stone occupied a spot in this section. The stones that did exist were sporadically positioned atop the many small hills that comprised the west side of the cemetery. From a distance they resembled sentinels guarding sacred ground.

Grandpa would ritualistically pull his truck up the short lane, stopping in front of the big wide gate. This was the sole entrance to Lost Mound. Without any prompting, my brother hopped out of the back of the truck to unfasten the rope that secured the gate. It was easy to see he had been through this drill a few times. John swung open the gate and then hopped back into the truck. Our grandfather then drove the big red truck loaded down with mowers and grandsons up the makeshift grass road. He parked his truck under a huge elm tree that sat on a small plateau overlooking the greater share of the cemetery. This spot represented the headquarters for his operations. Similar to a field commander in wartime, he began assessing the terrain to determine where he would deploy his troops for battle.

John Mason always manned the heavy artillery (riding mower). He was responsible for mowing the large football field area. Grandpa, with his self-propelled mower, would take care of the slopes that separated the high ground from the low ground. My brother John was assigned to the larger share of the high ground while I would do the remainder.

Once the mowers were lowered onto the grass, John Mason got the big riding mower going and took off. My brother John was next. Once my grandfather got his mower going, he went off to complete his assignment. I could now smell the scent of freshly cut grass. It spurred my anticipation as my itch to mow grew fiercely, but before I could, my grandfather had to get his mower going first. I watched him walk over to the pride of his fleet, the self-propelled mower. He adjusted a few controls on the mower and then gave a strong tug on the pull cord. It started right up. He then placed it in neutral and shifted his attention to my mower. Finally, it was my turn. That little mower I was using had one distinct ailment: it was hard to get started. I watched intently as my grandfather repeatedly alternated between working the choke and pulling the cord. I began to wonder if he could get it started at all, but then, right as the doubt entered my mind, the little mower turned over and a few breaths of exhaust puffed out from underneath the carriage. We both exhaled a sigh of relief as my moment arrived. Before sending me off, my grandfather issued a word of caution. Slowly removing the cigar from his mouth, he customarily cleared his throat before admonishing, "Now whatever you do, don't go in the tall grass, for it will clog up and I'll never get it started again." I acknowledged his instructions with a nod, but as soon as he was gone, my lust for lawn mowing glory got the best of me. I reasoned I could save time by cutting my way through the tall grass. I was certain I could pull it off. All I could think of was how impressed he'd be once he discovered how far ahead I was.

So off I headed, full steam, straight into the tall grass, and of course within a few short pushes the mower began to stall until finally coming to a sudden halt. My worst fears materialized. I had just done the unthinkable by deliberately disobeying his instructions. My mind began racing at a million revolutions per second. My first thought was if I acted quickly enough I could pull my mower out of the quagmire and get it started again before he came back. I quickly searched for a clearing, but out of the corner of my eye I noticed my grandfather approaching. When he discovered I had disobeyed his instructions my shoulders sunk. I then cringed as I heard the immortal words roll off his tongue, "Oh, you damn fool!" When you heard these words, you knew that things were as bad as they could possibly get. It was certainly a far cry from the physical and verbal abuse I would have taken had it been my father I had let down. In that moment I would have gladly taken a beating in exchange for eradicating my grandfather's disappointment in me.

As I agonized over what I had done, I prayed he wouldn't give up on me. Fortunately for me, this wasn't the case. He did give me a second chance. He managed to get the mower going again, and this time I learned my lesson by heeding his instructions without question. I carefully mowed my way around the tall grass before reaching my assigned area. Before it was over, I redeemed myself by accurately finishing my job on time.

I learned a lot that day. I vowed I'd never let him down again. Some years later he gave me the ultimate compliment by saying, "I think Jim has become a better mower than John." I never told my brother this, but I could not have been prouder. There was never a need for either of us to compete for our grandfather's favor. We knew it was an impossibility, for he always treated us as equals, which only furthered our admiration for him. He had become the father we never had.

Head for the Cellars!

One hot summer day my grandfather was out at the garden picking strawberries with my father and me. The three of us were intensely lost in our work when suddenly Grandpa stood up, looked at the sky, sniffed the air, and firmly said, "That's it. Let's go!" Uncharacteristically my father arose and instantly followed my grandfather's lead. Now I'm not sure which puzzled me more, my father's newfound unquestioned obedience or why we were leaving so abruptly. We had only been in the garden for an hour or so when Grandpa gave the order to leave. Despite this fact, we hopped in the red truck and headed back home. While driving home I learned my grandfather had sensed an approaching storm. I still failed to see the urgency in the matter, for the skies didn't appear threatening. Nevertheless, this was the reason for our hasty departure. Twenty minutes later we pulled into the driveway and started putting our fresh-picked produce away. Before entering the house I noticed the wind had picked up considerably. I stopped for a second to look at the sky. Its appearance reminded me of a child stricken with a severe case of jaundice.

When I got inside my house I peered out an open window only to see a sight I will never forget. An extremely large, dark, menacing cloud that stretched across the length of the horizon was fast approaching, blackening the entire sky as it came. It was so black it actually turned the day to night. Hypnotized by the sight, I stood frozen in awe. The wind gusts preceding this monstrosity began to send household objects flying through the air. Instinctively

I raised my arms to fend off the airborne debris. I then heard my grandfather yelling, "Head for the cellars! Head for the cellars!" It was too late for all of us in the house. The tempest was upon us. I heard my father screaming at us to kneel down and cover our heads. Unable to resist my curiosity, I lifted my head to look out the window. At that precise moment I witnessed the large maple tree that we had designated as the "interference tree" during the wiffle ball years snap in half like a toothpick. The top of the smaller oak tree that stood across from the maple was completely flat to the ground. I was terrified. Not even my father scared me this much.

Incredibly, it had left as fast as it had come. In the deafening silence we looked at each other in total shock. The finger of God had passed through our town, reminding us of just how frail our existence was. I no longer questioned why my father listened so obediently to my grandfather's words.

When we emerged from our home, I could scarcely believe the devastation that lay before me. Our neighbor's roof was sitting in our front yard. Dozens of huge trees had been reduced to a tangled pile of broken limbs. Cars had been tossed around like toys, and one was resting upside down. Power lines were strewn across streets with a few of them shooting off sparks as if it were their last breath. Broken glass was everywhere. Many windows in the homes on our block were either shattered or completely missing. The scene was one of utter devastation.

As I continued to survey the damage, I noticed my grandfather emerge from the protection of his cellar. Curiously, I didn't see my grandmother with him. During the calamity, his instinct for self-preservation had overtaken all other concerns. He was now running to the front door of his house to check on my grandmother. Seeing this unfold I quickly followed behind him praying for her safety. I came to a sudden stop when I saw my grandfather standing in front of his house talking to my grandmother at their front door. Thank God she was okay. Incredibly, for the duration of the storm she had stood directly in front of a plate glass window while watching the tornado pass through our tiny village. God himself must have protected her.

The tornado that hit Hanover on that June day in 1974 was the most frightening experience of my life. Old timers who lived in the area claimed it was impossible for a tornado to hit Hanover since it sat in a valley surrounded by hills. They believed if one did come, it would harmlessly bounce off the hills, bypassing the town altogether. In the Bible it states, "Thou shall not tempt your Lord God." Whether or not the old timers were tempting God or just being overconfident, the impossible did happen and everyone who endured the ordeal lived to tell about it. Not one life was lost. Perhaps this represented a measure of good coming from bad.

My father and I walked around the town to witness the aftermath of the storm firsthand. In just a few short blocks we saw some fantastic sights. Among these was an enormous tree stump that ended up on a neighbor's car, flattening it like a pancake. We saw trees of every size uprooted and juxtaposed in ways I never thought possible. We saw household items in places where they didn't belong. The loss of trees in our town was staggering. The before and after pictures of Hanover made it appear like two entirely different towns. Living through this terrifying ordeal made me rethink my value system. I thanked God for sparing the lives of my family and prayed he would never put me through another tornado. So far so good.

The Coach and Four

When I think of my immediate family, I tend to think of my brother first. This was partly due to him being the oldest, but also because we were brothers. I always looked up to him despite any shortcomings he may have had.

When John moved next door with my grandparents, it felt like he was more of a neighbor than a brother. My grandparents kept him very busy in church and school activities, which resulted in us spending less and less time together.

One exception to this trend was a memorable occasion when my grandparents invited me out to dinner at one of their favorite restaurants appropriately named The Coach and Four. I say appropriately because there were always four of us that went. That would typically be the grandparents, the lucky grandchild who was asked to go, and my brother John, who always went because he was now part of their family. For John, this was just one more example of good coming from bad.

As mentioned earlier in the book, I was the least favorite grandchild of my grandmother, so I was seldom asked to go. I can still remember how excited I was when they finally invited me. The Coach and Four was located forty-five minutes north of Hanover just across the state line in Wisconsin. It was late in the afternoon on a Saturday when the four of us drove out of Hanover in my grandfather's car.

I was on my best behavior for this was a once-in-a-lifetime opportunity for me. John, on the other hand, had made this pilgrimage countless times, so for him it was little more than a routine trip. John loved fun and games and one of his favorites was creating havoc with my grandparents' hearing. They had reached the point in their lives where both of them were practically deaf without the assistance of a hearing aid. In those days, hearing aids were not the technological wonders they are today. They had sensitive controls that, if not correctly set, would make a high-pitched whistling noise, alerting the user that an adjustment was needed.

My brother loved to exploit their disability. Whenever their hearing aids began to whistle, it became a signal for him to initiate a series of pranks that often led to sheer bedlam. He began by talking as loud as he could. This led my grandparents to believe that their hearing aids needed to be adjusted down. Then he would pretend to be talking by moving his lips while making no sound at all. They now adjusted their hearing aids back up. He repeated this tactic back and forth, creating so much confusion that you could see their faces become flustered as they tried in vain to find the proper setting. John, who was an excellent whistler, could perfectly mimic the high-pitched sound of their hearing aids to further their frustration. He continued this routine for another five minutes or so. By now I was desperately trying to contain my laughter but to no avail. Worried by the repercussions of what my grandmother would do should she suspect any involvement on my part, I struggled to regain my composure. After much pleading, I was able to convince my brother to cease his antics. To my relief, he finally gave in. Looking back at it all, it's no wonder he pursued a career in comedy. His love for laughter had been there from the very beginning.

Crossing Boundaries

One would think the combination of my father's reputation as a violent disciplinarian and having to bear witness to the abuse my brother John endured would have easily swayed any of us from ever trying anything. This held true for the most part, but there were times I went outside the lines. I remained ever cognizant of my father's volatile temper, but every so often a temptation would get the best of me.

When I was eleven years old, a friend of mine named Scott and I took up the hobby of coin collecting. We didn't have very much money to invest in our newfound hobby, but we discovered that collecting pennies and nickels was well within our reach. Lincoln wheatback pennies and older Jefferson nickels were still fairly common in circulation, so we began searching for these coins with a passion.

At the epicenter of our coin-collecting world was Maurice Jackson. Maurice was the owner of a small coin shop located on Main Street. He was a retired man who never seemed to tire of us kids bringing in our severely worn coins to be graded or priced. We could always count on finding Maurice sitting behind the counter of his shop reading the latest coin-pricing guide. He wore coke-bottle bifocal glasses that highlighted his bushy gray eyebrows. The withered lines that ran across his face concealed his gentle nature. Countless times I brought him worthless coins to look over, hoping beyond all hope I had found something rare and valuable. Inevitably he would respond with a patented phrase I had come to hear a thousand times over, "Hell, that thing couldn't buy you a cup of coffee!"

My quest to bring Maurice something spectacular reached its crest when Scott and I discovered the coin-changing machine at our local Laundromat. If you placed a quarter in the machine it would give back your change in nickels. We soon began saving our change and converting it into quarters. We then made our way down to the Laundromat to try our luck. We were amazed at the nickels we found. We even found an occasional buffalo head nickel.

On one such occasion to the Laundromat, Scott put a quarter into the machine, but it failed to return his change. He became infuriated and started banging on the coin return on top of the machine. After a few good whacks, a pile of coins poured out from the machine. The more we pounded the more the money came out. This was better than Vegas. We continued to take turns pounding on the machine. Before long our pockets were stuffed with coins. We built up quite an appetite from all the pounding and decided to go next door to the gas station and treat ourselves to a frozen candy bar and a soda. With each step we took a loud "shinging" noise preceded from our pockets. While enjoying our treats we began boasting over our newfound luck. Scott suggested we go back and clean out the machine. I made a mild protest, but greed got the best of me and we went back for more. Unfortunately, the owner of the gas station overheard us and promptly called the cops. It wasn't long before officer Ronnie Girot of the Hanover Police Department pulled up in his squad car directly in front of the Laundromat.

The guilty expressions on our faces confirmed the tip he had received from the gas station owner. He calmly told us, "You boys can either give me the money now or you can give it to me later, but if you give it to me now, I won't tell your parents." Without the least bit of hesitation we handed over the money. He told our parents anyway, and we caught hell for the stunt. I thought for sure I'd get a beating for this one, but fortunately for me my father had been under the weather, so he settled on threatening me within an inch of my life, swearing if he ever caught me hanging out with Scott again, he'd beat me senseless. His father told him the same thing—minus the threat. Within a week we were hanging out together again, but the real moral of the story was that crime doesn't pay.

A short time later another event that shook my world took place at my house. My father seldom took my mother with him when he went out drinking. In an uncharacteristic show of thoughtfulness, he decided she deserved a night out. The only problem was there was no one to watch the kids. Kerry couldn't because she was working. Without giving it a second thought he made a parental decision to leave me in charge of my two diabetic sisters. It's probably not necessary for me to mention how wrong it was to leave an adolescent in charge of two juvenile diabetics. But the old man's determination to take his wife out for a few drinks superseded any parental responsibilities. My mother protested, but he persuaded her by saying they were only going to the tavern downtown.

Before leaving, the only instruction my father gave me was under no circumstances were we to leave the yard. Once they were gone, it appeared as if the evening would be uneventful. Eydie was inside the house engaged in her favorite pastime, doing the dishes. Sara and I were outside playing when some of the neighbor kids happened by. They enticed us into playing a friendly game of freeze tag, which we obliged, providing we played in our yard. Shortly after we started, one of the local terror kids showed up, demanding we let him in the game. We reluctantly agreed. Shortly after play resumed, he became infuriated after being frozen several consecutive times. In a predictable display of anger he reached out for the closest thing to him and started shaking it violently. This turned out to be a big problem, for the outlet of his frustration was the metal gas line that ran from the gas tank to our house. Within a matter of seconds we all heard the alarming sound of gas hissing as it leaked from the broken line. The unmistakable scent of gas quickly permeated the air. Once everyone realized the seriousness of what had happened they began scattering like frightened rabbits with one kid yelling at the top of his lungs, "Take cover, it's gonna blow!" My mind started racing at a thousand miles per second. I remember asking myself, "What should I do? How could I stop it? What would my father do to me when he found out?"

For some unknown reason I remembered Eydie was still in the house. I bolted into the house screaming at her to get out fearing it might explode at any minute. Her actions were priceless. She was still doing the dishes when I alerted her to the danger. In one swift motion she placed the dirty dishtowel over her ears to muffle the sound of the potential explosion, as if this action would have made a difference. I couldn't help but laugh when I saw how ridiculous she looked.

My mind immediately returned to its preoccupied state with the catastrophe at hand. Out of nowhere a thought popped into my head, *Grandpa!* I made a wild dash for my grandparents' house next door. My feet were flying, my heart was pounding madly, and I was praying fervently, "God, please let him be home!" I reached the porch of his house. Frantically I opened the front door. Thank God, there was Grandpa sitting in his favorite chair eating chocolate-covered peanuts while watching his favorite television show, *Hee Haw.* My prayers were answered! In an instant I told him what happened. He arose from his chair and dashed across the yard with me trailing behind him. Once there he made his way over to the big gas tank in our yard. He shut the gas off at the source. He then asked me where my parents were. When I heard his question, the realization of what my father would do once he found out scared the living daylights out of me. Sheepishly, I told my grandfather they had gone downtown to the tavern for a few drinks.

My grandfather sent us back in our house while he returned to his house to call the tavern since we were without a phone. I then waited, silently dreading my father's arrival. A short time later a vehicle appeared in front of the house. One of his beer-drinking buddies had given him a lift home. Fully drunk, he came charging through the door calling out my name. I responded with a whimper as he met me in the living room. Raising his voice at me in a horrific display of anger he shouted, "I thought I left you in charge! What the hell happened?" I tried to explain, but before I could get the first few words out of my mouth, I was hit with a right cross to the jaw that literally sent me flying across the room. Slumped over in the corner, I actually saw stars circling above my head. It was like something out of a Bugs Bunny cartoon, except it wasn't funny. My dad then walked out of the house, jumped back in his buddy's car, and went back to the tavern. I'm not sure how long I sat there. The last thing I remember was being helped to bed by my sisters. This event marked the pinnacle of my father's use of violence against me. I don't ever recall being hit that hard again.

The "Two Girls"

Whenever I think of my two youngest sisters, I am reminded of how they always gave me their best. This was not limited to just the painful moments; it held true for the good times as well. They were extremely inventive when it came to filling in our spare time together. I'm sure this was partly due to the fact we owned few toys, so we had to rely on an ancient practice called "using your imagination." Wouldn't it be nice to see today's youth engage in this practice more often?

On any given afternoon we spent hours playing games like "store" and "house." My mother never had any objection to us emptying her cupboard of what few canned goods or packaged products that happened to be on hand, providing of course we picked up and put everything away before our father came home.

We would carry the grocery items into our bedroom to set up the store. I loved playing the role of the proprietor while the girls played the part of the customers. Many different scenarios were played out, which included customer complaints, customers who paid on credit, free groceries for the poor, and of course, the occasional shoplifting customer.

Playing house had many variations, but the most famous version was when my youngest sisters portrayed a married couple. I played the part of their baby boy who was appropriately named Magellan because of his relentless pursuit for exploration. Magellan often came up missing, causing his devoted parents much grief. I can't recall how many times they put Magellan down for a nap only to find his crib empty when they returned to check on him. I had a knack for hiding, so this gave me a chance to upset the apple cart. I loved listening to my sisters as they searched intently for their adventurous boy. Silently I waited for them to cry out in desperation the familiar words, "Magellan! Magellan! You bad baby, where are you? If you don't come out right away, you're going to get a spanking!" After they had screamed the name Magellan about forty more times, I would wait for them to leave the room and then sneak back into my bed as if I had never left. This combination of role playing and hide-and-seek kept us going for hours on end. I can't ever remember us tiring of it.

When my older sister Kerry entered high school, we were suddenly left with fewer ideas for fun. One summer we did our best to resurrect Kerry's famous yard carnival by putting one on ourselves. We successfully brought back many of the games she had incorporated in the old days. However, we faced a major obstacle in coming up with prizes for the kids who won the games. I had donated some of my baseball cards and between the three of us we had a little money to purchase some penny candy, but it wasn't nearly enough.

We were desperate for prizes, so we decided to search every inch of the house in hopes of finding something we could use. When all hope seemed lost, Eydie brought out a cardboard box containing a stockpile of her potholders she had crocheted over the years. Doubts entered my mind as to whether any kid would ever want such a prize, but desperate times breed desperate men, so we thought, *Why not?*

Once the carnival was in full gear, to my chagrin, kids were coming back in droves inquiring if we had more of those colorful potholders. It seemed the moms of the neighborhood had become enthralled by not only the durability of Eydie's designer potholders but also the myriad of brightly colored patterns they came in. The potholders I had once referred to as stupid were now the source of our success. I was the one who felt stupid now. I found myself apologizing to Eydie for ever making fun of those glorious potholders.

Branded by Innocence

As long as my father was away at work, my mother never deprived us of having fun. We must have driven her nuts with our imaginations, but you would have never known it. In return, we gave our complete allegiance to her; not that she demanded much, but every so often she did ask us to go to the store for her if the need arose. Since I was the man of the house, I often did the running for her.

On one such occasion I overheard my mom and older sister Kerry clandestinely discussing an urgent need that had arisen unexpectedly. She asked me to run an errand for her, and, of course, being a good son, I obliged. She handed me a few dollars and instructed me to go to the grocery store and pick up a large box of Kotex. Now at the time, I was about twelve, so I was completely clueless of what I was being asked to get. She simply told me where they were located in the store and that the box was very large and light purple in color. That was good enough for me. I hopped on my bike and took off down Main Street.

When I got to the grocery store it took me a few minutes before I found what I was looking for. As I came around an aisle in the store I spotted the large lavender-colored boxes sitting in a corner all by themselves. I reached over and picked one up. I then made my way to the checkout. Some of the other patrons in the store gave me a few peculiar looks, but I ignored them, wondering why on earth they were staring at me. After I had purchased the Kotex, an older gentleman who was bagging groceries offered me a bag. I reasoned they were already in a box, so I told him to save his bag for someone who really needed it.

When I got outside the store, I jumped on my bike and made my way back down Main Street with the big lavender Kotex box firmly secured under my arm. I didn't get too far when I noticed just about every car or truck that drove past me was emphatically honking their horn at me. By the time I was halfway home I was dumbfounded by all of the attention I was receiving. Some people were shouting out what sounded like obscenities while others simply made ludicrous gestures toward me. I was at a total loss as to why there was so much commotion over a big purple box.

When I finally pulled into my front yard, I hopped off my bike and delivered the goods. My mom saw me coming and said, "You didn't get a bag?" I said, "No, but I sure got a lot of attention on the way home. What are these things anyway?" She tried to conceal the smirk on her face, but I detected it. I then asked for an explanation. Obviously not wanting to continue the conversation, she merely said it was none of my business. My curiosity wasn't about to let her off the hook that easily. I persisted by demanding to know exactly what was inside the big purple box. She paused for a few moments and finally said, "It's a sanitary napkin!" My response was, "Oh," as if I knew what she was talking about. In reality I had no idea what that meant, but I knew by the tone of her voice I shouldn't ask again.

Innocence is a great thing. Some of us seem to lose it faster than others. For me, my innocence lasted longer than most, primarily due to a lack of parental instruction. I learned more from kids on the playground than I ever learned from my parents. From this dubious wealth of knowledge came plenty of misinformation that prolonged my naivety, at times to the point of embarrassment. Later on in life, I vowed to never let my own children be forced to rely on learning the lessons of the birds and bees in the same way I had.

The Garden Gets a Car

Time went on and my siblings and I were growing up. 1976 was a big year for the family because of two groundbreaking events. First, we finally got a telephone, so we were officially no longer isolated from the outside world. My father declined the long distance service, but at least it was now possible to actually have a conversation with a friend on the phone. Technology was never more appreciated.

The second life-changing event in 1976 happened when my father purchased his first vehicle. Initially, this generated great excitement for those of us who were still at home. My father's choice of vehicle was a large black and orange Ford van. We could not have been happier with his choice. The first time he pulled up in front of the house, we cheered! The van was spacious and included two rows of bus seats for the kids as well as two comfortable captains' chairs for my parents.

Within a week our cheers turned to sneers when our father pulled up in front of the house one rainy afternoon. The bus seats we had recently jumped for joy over were gone. He had them removed so he could haul his produce from his garden. From a priority standpoint this was a "no-brainer" for him. From our standpoint, we had taken a back seat, or should I say no seat at all to the needs of his garden. The inside of the van had been reduced to a hollow empty shell. The two captains' chairs were all that remained. The only thing in the back of the van was the raised metal tracking that ran along the length of the floor bed. My mother actually complained for the first time in years by retorting, "Where are the kids going to sit?" My father's solution was simple. "We'll just lay a couple of old blankets down whenever the kids come along."

To demonstrate the feasibility of his plan he offered to take the entire family out to the movies in Dubuque. The movie *Jaws* had just come out and, at the time, it was a box office smash. My sisters and I soon forgot about the seats being yanked out. The thrill of just being able to do something outside of our home far outweighed the compromise of not having a seat to sit on. Or so we thought.

It normally took about forty-five minutes to get to Dubuque, but since my father had only recently learned to drive, he seldom exceeded fifty miles an hour on the open road. Meanwhile, it wasn't far into the trip when we began to feel the effects of the raised metal tracking on our tender derrières. We had been on the road less than ten minutes when we realized we were in for a torturous ride. No matter how often we repositioned ourselves, the bumps kept coming.

Peering out the back of the van window, I noticed a caravan of cars helplessly stuck behind my pokey father. The highway that ran from Hanover to Dubuque was hilly and curvy, making it almost impossible for a vehicle to pass. In an attempt to take my mind off my sore bottom, I started counting the vast number of cars trapped behind us. I glanced up front and saw my father with a death grip on the wheel, infrequently looking back at the line of cars in his rearview mirror. A few seconds later I heard him raise his voice in disgust saying, "Damn tailgaters!" My poor mother looked at me and shook her head, but like me, she dared not say a word.

Relieved to have finally reached Dubuque, my sisters and I slowly crawled out of the van. We had ridden most of the way in a crouched position with knees fully bent. The three of us had a lot of trouble straightening up. We resembled three children stricken with polio, but we were still smart enough not to complain too loudly for fear of our father overhearing us. Those seats in the movie theater were a sight for sore eyes. Once the stiffness wore off we were able to enjoy the movie but dreaded the thought of the drive back home. It had become painfully obvious to us that this would be our first and last family adventure in the van.

Growing Pains

With the onset of my high school years, the three remaining children still in the home were now teenagers. By this point, one might think that my father's perverse behaviors would have begun to mellow a bit. If anything, it was quite the contrary. He maintained his torrid drinking while his trademark qualities of insensitivity, self-centeredness, and neglectfulness became further entrenched.

On rare occasions he would purchase a twelve pack and bring it home for a night of family bonding. The highlight of these evenings usually included several room-clearing beer farts and an occasional session of toenail clipping. Fortunately for us, my father only clipped his toenails a few times a year. In one respect this was a blessing, for it limited the number of times we were exposed to the spectacle. On the other hand, by prolonging it, he made a nasty task even more repulsive. His toenails were yellow and hard as acrylic. The sheer sound generated by clipping one was deafening. Worse yet, the dagger-like projectiles were sent hurtling through the air only to end up lodged somewhere in our shag carpeting. These clippings became deadly booby traps waiting to be sprung by the tender foot of an unsuspecting child. The days that followed could only be described as hellish. It was reminiscent of U.S. marines dodging punji-sticks in the jungles of Vietnam.

Around this same time my father traded in his nicotine habit for tobacco chewing. On those nights when he would come home, drinking and tobacco chewing were done hand in hand. Generally upon the completion of his first beer, he would convert the empty can into a makeshift spittoon so he had a means of chewing without having to leave his perch on the cot. Whenever he needed a fresh Hamm's beer he simply barked at my mother to bring him a replacement, and like a faithful servant, she would instinctively fetch it on command. She even popped the top so it was ready for instant guzzling. His empire had reached its pinnacle.

One evening after drinking many rounds he bellowed to our mother, "Woman! I'm thirsty! Get me a fresh beer!" With lightning speed she rushed in and set a freshly opened Hamm's beer can among the plethora of empties he had consumed earlier. After a hearty first chug he set down his beer and returned his attention to the television show he had been watching. After a few minutes passed, he assumingly reached for his beer but instead grabbed the can he'd been using for his spittoon. He took a healthy swallow and upon doing so immediately gasped! We turned around and watched him turn from white as a ghost to green as a swamp. Gagging from the foul contents, he flew off his cot and dashed into the bathroom where he promptly vomited. I won't lie, my sisters and I took great satisfaction in his suffering, but we were careful to hide our enjoyment. We knew any display of disloyalty would be met with swift retaliation. Our mom wisely sent us off to bed in fear of him taking it out on us. This is a great example of how my mother became adept at staying one step ahead of my father's explosive temper. She had been exposed to his cruel ways for so long that her reactions had become instinctual. It was a by-product of a bizarre marriage.

Fortunately, once I entered high school the opportunities for me to participate in these special moments of family bonding became less and less frequent. This was partly due to finding a job, but I also became involved in a number of the extracurricular programs my school offered such as drama club, speech team, and of course several sports including baseball, basketball, and track. My popularity with my peers grew, but my appearance remained a thorn in my side. I was still working for my grandfather in the summers, but I didn't make enough to afford all of the clothes I needed. I knew there was no possibility of my father helping, so I took matters into my own hands by looking for a steady job after school.

My sister Kerry, who had faced the same dilemma as I, landed a job at one of the local grocery stores, Bill's Royal Blue. The job vastly improved her situation, which ultimately opened a door for me as well when she volunteered me to help out with the store's annual inventory. I made the most of the situation by working my tail off. My hard work paid off, for within a short time Bill Wolters, the owner, offered me a job bagging groceries. I was pretty excited when I earned my first paycheck. Within a few weeks I had saved enough to purchase some new clothes. My confidence started to rise. What a difference a few good clothes made!

Later on I went to work for Whistling Wings. They raised and distributed mallard ducks all over the United States. This franchise made Hanover the "Mallard Capital of the World." I must admit I wasn't entirely sure what the position entailed. I started out in the hatchery that was located in town. I was informed my main duty would be shoveling the inexhaustible supply of guano that was generated by the hatchlings. There were many pens set up with young ducks of different ages. The ducklings remained at the hatchery until they were close to flying. Once they reached adulthood they were moved to one of the big farms that Whistling Wings owned outside of town.

It didn't take me long to graduate from my "guano-chucking" responsibilities. One day I was informed by my boss that I would now report to one of the farms in the country where the mature ducks were kept. This was a huge opportunity for me because it gave me a chance to drive on a regular basis. I had my driver's license before I ever went to work for Whistling Wings, but my father was unwilling to let me practice with his van, which made driving opportunities scarce. I can still remember the day they asked me if I had my driver's license. I proudly answered yes, and they flipped me the keys to the old red truck that sat out in front of the hatchery. I was instructed to drive out to the main farm and locate Mr. Don, who would instruct me on my new duties.

Thrilled beyond words, I jumped into the truck ready to prove my driving prowess. However, my surging confidence quickly evaporated when I discovered the truck had a manual transmission. I had never driven a stick shift before, but I wasn't about to let this stand in the way of my one chance to drive. So I did what I normally did in situations like this. I forged full speed ahead. I knew the basic workings of a stick shift and felt pretty sure I could do it. Lucky for me it was a three speed, which made the shifting a little easier to figure out. The only problem I had was finding reverse. After grinding the gears a few times, I opted for the old standby solution of letting the vehicle roll back in neutral, thus avoiding reverse all together. Once I got on the open road I picked it up pretty fast, and before long I was driving that truck like an old pro.

In the fall of that year I became a junior in high school. The upgrades I had made to my appearance helped me gain the backbone for approaching the opposite sex. One girl with whom I became involved kept asking me to invite her over to my house. She was curious about my home life. Ashamed for obvious reasons, I postponed the invite for as long as I could, but she persisted. Over time, I reluctantly gave in. After agreeing to have her over, I told her I'd give her a call and set up an evening for her to come over.

In the nights that followed I made sure my father completed his predictable routine of coming home, eating dinner, and vacating for the tavern. The first night everything went according to plan. The old man headed down to his cave right on schedule, but unfortunately she was unable to come over. She did tell me that any other night of the week would be fine. The next night my dad remained true to form, leaving shortly after supper. As soon as he left I called her and arranged for her to come over. I told my mother I was going over to her house to pick her up and would be returning shortly for a visit.

I wasted no time in getting up to her house, doing my best not to break a sweat. When I arrived she commented on the speed at which I had gotten there on foot. I told her I was anxious to see her, which made her smile. Inside, I was still apprehensive about her coming over, even if my father wasn't there. Our house looked like an old beat-up shack compared to the beautiful, well-furnished home she lived in. This fact worried me, for I feared she'd think less of me once she saw how primitively I lived. I told myself there wasn't a whole lot I could do about it except to try to keep the visit as brief as possible.

When we rounded the corner to my house, I froze dead in my tracks. There, parked in front of the house, sat my father's van! She sensed the change in my demeanor and said, "What's wrong?" I shrugged off her question with an "Oh nothing," even though my worst fears had just materialized before my very eyes.

Acknowledging that there was no turning back now, we made our way up the steps to my house. Upon entering there sat my dad at the kitchen table, drinking a Hamm's beer while reading one of his gardening manuals. When we entered the front door he looked up and said in a curious voice, "Well... who's this cute girl you brought home? Jim, get over here and let me smell your fingers!" I nearly died. Right before my very eyes I watched her turn several shades. Her face looked a lot like my father's on the night he swallowed his own chew spit.

At least I had gotten my wish for a short visit. Mortified by what had just taken place, we abruptly left. To say the least, the walk back to her house was a little awkward. It was clearly obvious that there would be no good coming from bad here. Soon after this embarrassing episode she dumped me, and our short-lived romance came to a sudden end. I never brought another girl home for the rest of my high school years.

You're on Your Own Now

A little more than a year later I graduated from high school. I had a short-term plan for my future, but before initiating it my father told me he had something for me. I thought, *Wow, could it be a graduation gift?* Even if it was only a little money, I could surely put it to good use. I actually got a little excited wondering what he was going to do for me.

When I arrived home he heard me enter the house. He immediately called out for me from the living room. In his usual deep voice he said, "Come in here. I have something for you." I thought; *This is it!* When I joined him in the living room I patiently waited for him to hand me something, but instead he said, "I've got some advice for you." My body slumped forward as the words rolled off his tongue. He went on to say, "There are five things you need in life. The first is water, the second is food, the third is clothing," but before he told me the fourth and fifth revelations, I was so disappointed I lost interest. Then, he ended his words of wisdom with, "I got you this far. You're on your own now!"

I left home the day after my graduation. A good friend named Bob, who happened to be a coworker of mine at Bill's Royal Blue, was well aware of my forthcoming graduation from high school. He offered me a way out of Hanover, and more importantly, a way out of my father's house. He had been attending college in nearby Morrison, Illinois. He also worked as a manager in a local grocery store there. He told me they were looking for stockers on their night crew, and if I was interested, he could get me on. He also offered to share his apartment with me. Bob was fully aware of my circumstances. He did everything in his power to help me out, including basing the cost of my room and board on proportional income. He would be the first in a long line of friends who gradually helped me out of my hole and on the path to a somewhat normal way of life.

The first night in my new surroundings was one I will never forget. My room was very small, but Bob had furnished it with a bed, a lamp, and a nightstand. Shortly after we went to bed that night, I experienced true peace for the first time in my life. All was calm. Living in an environment absent of fear was an unfamiliar feeling to me. The permanent dark cloud that had hung over me my entire life had been suddenly lifted. The impossibility of my father barging into my room in a drunken rage was almost too much to comprehend. I will never forget that feeling for as long as I live. My only regret was that I couldn't do the same for my two younger sisters. They remained trapped in the hell from which I had fled. That night, in the security of my new surroundings, I vowed to do everything in my power to rescue Eydie and Sarah from the same fate I had escaped.

Death Comes Knocking

Moving to Morrison was the first step in my quest to achieve self-sufficiency. Over the next three years I bounced around towns in northern and central Illinois working for several different grocery store chains. I saved everything I could until I was able to afford a reliable car.

By 1982, I had worked my way up into one of the largest grocery store chains in Peoria, Illinois. I was clearing about $250 dollars a week, which at the time was a decent wage for a single guy. I lived in my own apartment that was located less than twenty minutes from work. I had been working this job for a little more than a year. All in all life was much better with the exception of one thing—the "graveyard shift." It was one of the few drawbacks to working in this industry. Entry-level employees were required to start out on third shift. After a few years of loyal service, they would earn the right to a position on either first or second shift.

Having no say in the matter, I went about the task at hand, confident I could ride out the overnights.

Sometime during my second year of employment the effects of working third shift began to take a heavy toll on me. To make things worse I developed insomnia and found it almost impossible to sleep during the day. Seldom did I drop off before dinner, which meant I slept right up until it was time to go to work. This greatly added to my stress as I often woke up just minutes before it was time to go to work. After several incidences of showing up late, I was fired for excessive tardiness.

I was obviously devastated by this sudden turn of events. I never planned on losing my job. Worse yet, I didn't have a backup plan either. The country was in a recession, so finding a new job was virtually impossible. Earlier in the story I spoke of my brother's reaction to my dilemma. He was actually thrilled to hear I had lost my job. I found it a little hard to rejoice in the matter, but he assured me if I moved up to Dubuque everything would work out. When I arrived in Dubuque, I couldn't help feeling like a dog with its tail tucked between its legs.

By no means did moving to Dubuque solve my job problems. One huge obstacle lying in my path was the unemployment rate in Dubuque. It was over forty percent! I knew our country had fallen on hard times, but I never realized I had placed myself smack dab in the middle of the highest unemployment rate in the country. Things were now looking bleak with no relief on the horizon. John told me not to pay attention to the unemployment rate. He'd say, "Statistics are for idiots. If you have a job, then the unemployment rate is zero, if you don't have a job, then it's 100 percent." I couldn't argue his point. My concern was how long would it remain at 100 percent.

John's job as a physician's assistant was more than adequate to foot the bills until I could find a job. Shortly before I came to Dubuque he had rejoined the ranks of bachelorhood. His wife Debbie and daughter Sarah had moved back to California a little less than a year ago. The divorce had been very hard on him. He seemed more than willing to make a few sacrifices if it meant having a little family around. I still couldn't help feeling that my life had taken a turn for the worse. I tried to stay positive by reminding myself of the old spiritual philosophy of: "This too shall pass."

My job prospects remained unfruitful for a few months. Despite this, my spirits were high, for being with John seemed to diminish the seriousness of my predicament. We played on a softball team together, talked Cubs baseball constantly, and did quite a bit of partying together. However, looking back on it all, I had no idea how unforeseen events made my move to Dubuque even more meaningful than I could have ever imagined.

Grandma's Death

Shortly after John and I returned home from our unforgettable trip out West, a frightening incident occurred involving our grandmother. While out for an evening stroll she fell, striking her head against the cement sidewalk. She also injured her arm and leg in the process. She was rushed to Dubuque where they diagnosed her with a severe concussion. Her injuries greatly limited her mobility. She now had to use a walker to get around. The family breathed a collected sigh of relief, for it could have been obviously much worse. Her doctors told us that her injuries were recoverable, providing she refrained from taking endangering walks.

She followed her doctor's orders for almost a year without further incident. In the summer of 1984, John and I were making regular visits to Hanover to see her as well as the rest of the family. Things seemed to be going well until she decided to ignore her doctor's advice. She started taking evening strolls without her walker. It wasn't long before she fell again. This time it was much more serious than before. Once again she was rushed to Dubuque, but this time it appeared her luck had run out. The family braced itself for the outcome.

When it happened, John found out before me. Upon hearing the news, he immediately rushed to her side. He called my work, telling them to notify me as soon as possible. I had recently started working as a delivery and set-up man for a waterbed store. When the incident took place, I was out of town on a delivery in southern Wisconsin. This was still prior to the cell phone era, so I was unaware of what had happened until I returned to the store. When I found out, I made a beeline for the hospital, which was located only a few miles away from my work.

Her doctors assessed her chances for recovery as being scant at best. We all knew how tough she was, and for that reason none of us discounted the possibility of her making a recovery. However, this time the concrete had clearly won. The blow she received from her fall sent her into a semi-comatose state. She appeared conscious, but it was quite apparent her faculties had left her. Her eyes were open, but she was unable to recognize anyone in her family, not even Grandfather. She could talk, but what came out was nothing more than incoherent gibberish.

When I arrived at the hospital I quickly made my way through the main doors. I stopped at the information desk to get the number of her room. The nurse directed me to the elevator and I made it just in time as the doors were about to close. When I reached her floor, the anxiety of not knowing what was happening started to turn my stomach. The elevator bell chimed and the doors opened.

Finding her wasn't very difficult. I immediately recognized a huge contingent of family members pacing outside a door. Their concerned faces told the whole story. This did not look good. I saw John coming out of her room. He spotted me right away. He quickly filled me in on everything. There wouldn't be any miracles this time. I told him I wanted to see her.

While entering her room, I glanced at some of the family members. Their sullen faces reaffirmed how bleak the situation was. Surely this was the end. Leading the way, John escorted me to her side. She was propped up in bed with her eyes open. She gave new meaning to the old phrase, "The lights are on, but nobody's home." As I moved closer to her I reached for her arm, but before I touched her, she cocked her head to one side, looked me straight in the eye, and said, "Jim! When are you going to get a haircut?" Everyone in the room was stunned when they heard her speak my name. Looks of total disbelief were plastered over their faces, for she had been unable to recognize any of her closest loved ones. But I, the least of her loved ones, had for a short moment brought her back from the depths of dementia.

She returned to her incoherent state almost as fast as she had come out of it. Evidently the sight of me ignited one final brain synapse that only my presence could have triggered. I shook my head, thinking it was only fitting she gave me hell one last time. Since everyone in the family was more than familiar with my grandmother's dislike for me, they found this incident extremely humorous and, if nothing more, cleared the gloomy atmosphere for a few brief moments.

While everyone enjoyed a hearty laugh at my expense, I began experiencing a series of childhood flashbacks that encapsulated my grandmother's dislike for me. She never once raised a hand to any of us kids, but there was little doubt as to who was the least favored grandchild. It became abundantly clear I was struggling with her life rather than death.

The first flashback I experienced in that moment returned me to a time when I couldn't have been more than four or five years old. I was walking across our yard with my hands in my pockets when at the exact same time my grandmother happened to be coming across the yard to our house. When she spotted me, she shot me a scornful look and then, in a harsh voice, ordered me to get my hands out of my pockets. I promptly obeyed, but was unsure as to why she wanted me to remove my hands from my pockets. As she passed by me she hissed, "You're disgusting!" I didn't have a clue as to what had just happened. It wasn't until years later that I realized she had suspected me of playing "pocket pool." I was more than a little taken back. I mean, I was a little kid. I didn't even know what "pocket pool" was! From an early age it became obvious she had it in for me, but I had no idea as to why.

My grandmother's love remained elusive during my younger years. By the time I became a teenager, my determination to win her over had become an obsession. Deep down inside I feared she could never allow herself to love me in the same way she had loved the rest of her grandchildren. Doubts like these only strengthened my resolve to win her over. By the time I reached high school, John had left for the service. His absence briefly opened a door, allowing me to get closer to her than I had ever been able to before.

I started showing up at her house every day after school. Slowly the bond we never had began to form. Without being asked, I started helping out around her house by doing odd jobs. Slowly she began to open up to me. We were suddenly spending more time together than all of our previous years combined. It took a lot of effort, but I began to win her over. For the first time we were really connecting. I felt we had done the impossible by sharing genuine moments together. It was one of the best feelings I ever had.

Sadly, the demands of high school and working a job made it difficult for me to sustain our newfound relationship. Despite the gains we had made, the demands on my personal time began to compromise our bond. It wasn't long before we started drifting apart again.

After graduation, I left home and we became even more distanced by the miles that separated us. I returned home on the weekends once or twice a month, but things were never the same. At least I could take some satisfaction in knowing that for a short while we experienced the "bond that never was."

As she lay in her hospital bed, the realization of her life coming to an end resurfaced all of those old feelings of unfinished business. I kept tormenting myself by replaying the "what if" card over and over again in my head. I wondered if I had given her more of my time could things have turned out a little different for us.

It wasn't until much later in life that I finally learned the true reason as to why she withheld her love for me. The truth came in the form of my uncle Jim. He told me two stories that finally shed light on this subject. The first occurred at the time when I was no more than three years old. It involved a seemingly harmless subject, chocolate chip cookies. One sunny afternoon my grandmother had been baking chocolate chip cookies when my brother John caught wind of the irresistible aroma. Once John picked up the scent, he immediately ventured over to my grandparents' house where he was rewarded with one of her delicious cookies. When my sister Kerry noticed John eating a cookie, she quickly put two and two together and made a wild dash to Grandma's house. When Eydie saw Kerry's cookie, she in turn made her way across the yard to get a cookie. It wasn't long before I noticed Eydie eating her cookie, so I followed suit and made my way across the yard to get a cookie. This is where the story gets interesting. My uncle Jim witnessed his mother's joy abound as in succession she watched her grandchildren traipsing across the yard to retrieve her cookies. My grandmother commented to him on how adorable it was to see each of us coming over one by one in hot pursuit of her cookies. That is, of course, until I came across her yard. When she spotted me high-tailing it over to her house, she gestured to my uncle and said, "Look, here comes the big boob!"

When I first heard this story I must admit it hurt. The truth can do that to you. My uncle went on to tell me the second story, which in comparison to the first story was like being hit with an atomic bomb. About a year before I was born, there were rumors of my parents engaging in the ancient practice of "wife swapping." Details are sketchy at best, but during the late 1950s, this practice had gained considerable exposure to mainstream America, and my parents supposedly acted on this taboo with another couple from town. It didn't take long for my grandparents to learn of the alleged sexual exploits of my parents. In the eyes of my grandmother, infidelity at any level would have been regarded as nothing short of appalling. When I arrived a year later, she became convinced I was not of my father's seed. In her eyes my ancestral legitimacy would forever remain in question, and now you know the rest of the story.

Knowing my grandmother's strict adherence to godly instruction, she must have had a *cow* over this one. I'm sure that if only for reasons of posterity, it would have been impossible for her to have reconciled this revelation. When I heard this story, years of wonderment dissolved, yet there were still questions that lingered. Such as, "Even if I wasn't of my father's seed, how could one who possessed such godly qualities take out their aggression on a defenseless child? Was she punishing me or my parents?" These and other troubling questions will forever remain unanswered.

My uncle reassured me by telling me there wasn't even a residual doubt as to whether or not I was my father's child. He added, "You have as much or more of your father's physical features and mannerisms than any of your siblings." I agreed, but I still struggled with my grandmother's treatment of me. I settled on the notion that it was her commitment to God's values that prevented her from giving her full love to me. One of the few human beings I had always revered as being the furthest removed from sin appeared to have at least one flaw.

A few days later my grandmother died peaceably in her sleep. She was the unquestionable matriarch of our family. She commanded respect and received it from everyone in her family. She had never backed down to anyone or anything. Her strong spiritual ideals formed the precepts that bonded the extended family into a single unit. This included my aunts, uncles, and cousins who remained loyal to her authority until the day she died. With her passing, this bond no longer existed in the same way as it had before her death. The things that are lost with a life never cease to amaze me.

The enormous turnout at her funeral confirmed the profound impact her godly life had on family and friends. She stood for so many things, but if there was any one word that could sum up her life it would be *righteousness.* Anyone who was acquainted with her knew that the Bible had the final word in everything she did. She was a true disciple of Christ, whose biblical convictions could only be described as exemplary.

Several stormy days preceded her death, but on the day of her funeral, bright sunshine pierced the dreary skies, as if signaling her entrance to heaven. I calmly watched as her body was lowered into the ground at the New Cemetery in Hanover. During those years when I was younger, I recalled mowing these same grounds, never once thinking I would return to them to see my own family buried there. Odd as it sounds, the cemeteries were always a happy place for me. I had always cherished the memories I had of mowing with my grandfather and brother. Despite all of the irony, deep down it remained a place of comfort.

My brother and I returned to Dubuque later that day. The first part of the trip back was very quiet. The silence was finally broken when we started reminiscing about the good old days of mowing in the cemeteries. For a brief moment this diverted our attention from Grandma's death. Our conversation eventually drifted to my grandfather. We promised each other right then and there that we would take time to visit him and never take him for granted.

A Day at the Races

For the most part, we kept our promise to our grandfather. Once or twice a month we made sure to drive down to Hanover to visit him. On one such occasion, the three of us took a trip into Chicago to play the horses at Arlington Race Track. My grandfather loved horse racing, and over the years he had made numerous trips to Arlington. He wasn't much of a gambler, but he loved the atmosphere. Seldom did he ever spend more than a couple of bucks on a race, but I can distinctly recall being mesmerized by his racetrack savoir-faire. He would walk around searching for an ideal seat to study his program. Once he found his spot, he would customarily pull out a thick, stinky cigar. After igniting his stogie, you could watch his eyes switching back and forth from his program to the ever-changing odds board. Just like an old pro, it was virtually impossible to distinguish him from the rest of the racetrack junkies.

When post time for a race drew near, you could watch the excitement build on his face. I think I got more enjoyment out of him than the actual race. Prior to the start of each race, he would walk down to where the horses were being paraded out in front of the crowd. He then meticulously studied the contenders before ever placing a wager. Jockey and horse were suited in brightly colored shades of green, red, yellow, purple, or orange. As soon as the overhead announcer informed the crowd the horses were being put into the starting gate, my grandfather, along with the rest of the hardcore gamblers, made a frantic dash for the betting windows. By the urgency of his approach you would have thought he had the mortgage to his house riding on the outcome of the next race.

Once his bet was placed, I could see his eyes begin to twinkle with anticipation. He would march down as close to the rail as he could possibly get while patiently waiting to hear the track announcer shout out the immortal words, "And ... they're off!" In a flash the gate was sprung. The herd of horses thundered down the track, kicking dirt high into the air as they passed us by. With precision blows the jockeys urged on their steeds by furiously striking the rump of each animal. In a desperate attempt to coax out a little more "giddy up," you could see the jockeys frantically kicking their feet inside their stirrups. The crowd cheered as the horses headed into the first turn. I looked over at my grandfather, he was searching in vain to find out where his horse was positioned in the pack. Typically his horse was in the back, but that didn't stop him from cheering him on. The announcer informed the crowd they had passed the final turn and then yelled those unmistakable words, "Down the stretch they come!" My grandfather's adrenaline rush reached its climax, despite the fact his horse was lagging far behind. Once the horses crossed the finish line he would ceremoniously smack his racing program against his other hand and shout out in disgust, "That worthless old nag never had a chance!" John and I struggled to withhold our laughter, for we knew this was serious business for him.

Seeing my grandfather removed from his normally calm, God-fearing way of life was to say the least a contradiction. As far as I know, horse racing and cigar smoking were the only vices he ever had. These indulgences demonstrated how even he was not impervious to sin. I think he only cashed in once or twice that day, but making money seemed less important than being in the winner's circle. All three of us left Arlington as losers, but in reality we were big winners, for the memories we forged far out valued any monetary gains.

The End of an Era and the Beginning of a New One

It was during this time that I fell into what I thought was love and, subsequently, fathered the first of my three children. Tyler was born in 1985. For me there was no greater joy than being a first-time father. He was a bright-eyed, bushy-tailed, healthy, and happy young boy who was everything a father could hope for. His sister, Mallory, who was just as beautiful and equally precious, was born in 1986.

Their births occurred out of wedlock. In all the years I spent in my first relationship, eleven in all, I never married. It seemed we could never be at the same point at the same time. Perhaps it was outside forces at work beyond our control; I'll never know. The one thing I did know was that I never wanted to be separated from my children.

Tyler was due in April. For a while I kept the pregnancy from my family. I was fearful of their reaction to me fathering a child out of wedlock. I was distraught over how I would break the news, but at least my grandmother was spared any shame. I was, however, concerned how my grandfather would take it. He ended up finding out on his own, and to my complete surprise, he was happy, not judgmental. My father, on the other hand, looked past the joy of another grandson by insisting the only thing that mattered was that I get married soon. I found it strange seeing him of all people taking a stance on morality. He seemed so far removed from his advice.

Shortly before Tyler was born, the State of Iowa built a brand new greyhound racing track in Dubuque. Several hundred jobs came available, so I put my hat in the ring hoping to get hired. I survived three intense rounds of interviewing before eventually earning a position as a teller. It was definitely a step up in pay, not to mention how relieved I was to be out of the waterbed delivery business. With the recent arrival of my son, the timing of this good fortune could not have come at a better time. Things were certainly looking up.

Tyler was only a month old when I took him to Hanover for his first visit. At this point my grandfather had yet to lay eyes on him. I couldn't wait to introduce him to his newest great-grandson. When we arrived, just like any newborn child, Tyler was smothered in attention by my mother and sisters. My grandfather had received prior notice of our coming. My sisters told me he was due home at any time. Almost immediately after they had told me this I spotted my grandfather pulling up in his truck. When he got out he came across our yard with a determined pace. I watched in great anticipation as he made his way to our front door. It was clear he wanted to see the child. I'm not sure which of us was more excited. As soon as he came inside, I handed him his new great-grandson. When he laid eyes on Tyler, an ear-to-ear smile came over his face. Uncharacteristically, he loudly proclaimed, "Now that's a crackerjack if I ever saw one!" Instantly a connection took place. Although Tyler was his fourth great-grandchild, none of us had ever seen him react like this. It was a moment I will always treasure.

A few weeks later I returned to Hanover for a family reunion. When I arrived with Tyler, it didn't take long before my grandfather started up his praise. As he carried on about Tyler, it was easy to see that the rest of the relatives were getting a little tired of hearing about it. Even I became embarrassed by his excessive admiration for Tyler. When everyone else got quiet he let up for a bit. However, a short time later when everyone was enjoying the meal, he started up again by saying, "Have you ever seen a baby like Jim's before? He's a true blue jim-dandy crackerjack if I ever saw one!" Immediately the relatives responded by rolling their eyes with that "here we go again look" on their faces. Unfortunately, it didn't deter his gloating one bit. Despite the awkwardness of his blatant adoration, I have to admit I could not have been prouder.

Kerry had been married for a number of years. She had two children of her own, a boy named Joshua and a girl named Amanda. She and her family were living in my grandparents' home. They had purchased the home from my grandfather shortly after my grandmother had passed away. The big old house was too much for him to take care of on his own. Deep down I think it pained him too much to continue living alone in the house in which he had spent so many years with the love of his life. I think he decided it would be better served if Kerry and her growing family lived there instead. He eventually sold it to her for a fair price. He moved into a recently built housing complex for the retired on the south side of town.

In July of that same year, John and I came up with the idea of taking Grandpa out to the dog track. It was no Arlington, but we were sure he'd get a big kick out of it. I had planned to go back to

Hanover that weekend, so I told John I'd arrange for him to come out to the track one night soon.

While driving down to Hanover, about halfway through the trip I saw what looked like my grandfather's car coming at me from the opposite direction. I was tempted to stop and turn around, but I wasn't completely sure if it was him, so I continued on to Hanover hoping it was just a car that looked like his.

Once I got to Hanover, I drove directly to my parents' house and asked my mom if she knew what my grandfather was up to. With a surprised look on her face she told me he was on his way to see me. I told her I thought I had seen him on the highway coming the other way. I was now wishing I would have followed my instinct. I told my mom of our plans to invite him up to the dog track. Despite our unfortunate timing, I told myself I'd drive back down next week.

By midsummer the novelty of dog racing was building momentum at an astounding rate. In July, a new purse record was set. Every weekend the purses were bigger than the one before. No one could have predicted the success the racetrack was enjoying during its inaugural season. Unfortunately, this same success forced me to postpone my plans to get Grandpa up to the track. John and I decided it would be more enjoyable for him if we waited until the tourist season died down.

The end of the month was fast approaching; it was July 30, and we were ridiculously busy for a weekday. I sat, perched at my window, shooting out ticket after ticket to what seemed like an infinite line of gamblers. By the time the tenth race arrived, I was exhausted. Before post time was called for the eleventh race, Henry, one of the money room attendants, informed me I was to report to the manager's office right away. He wouldn't say why.

Perplexed, I locked up my moneybox and made my way to the manager's office.

When I entered the office of the track manager, he bluntly informed me that my grandfather had passed away. The only thing I can remember was being completely shell-shocked by his words. I recall shouting out, "No, it can't be!" I slumped over as if every bit of life had been sucked from my body. I felt sick to my stomach. It took a few moments for me to collect myself. Once I did, I left the track and went home.

During the drive home I felt completely numb. I couldn't believe he was gone. I thought back to my recent visit to Hanover when I had passed him on the road. That was the last time I ever saw him alive.

John and I struggled mightily with his passing. We remained quiet about it for the most part. There really wasn't much to say. We felt empty. He was much more than just our grandfather. He was a dad, mentor, and role model. We knew more than just a legend had passed. There would never be another like him. I called my mother the next day. We kept talking about how no one had even the slightest inkling that his health was in jeopardy. She kept telling me, "For a man of eighty-four years, he was still in great shape." Everyone in the family felt he easily had another five or ten years left in him. It seemed impossible for him to just up and die.

My sister Kerry was there the day he complained of chest pains. She rode with him in the ambulance to the hospital. She told me it was the first time she had ever seen fear on his face. She told me he knew what was happening. I prayed for her, knowing how hard it must have been to be there in his dying moment.

The greatest man I ever knew was dead of a heart attack at the age of eighty-four. Kerry was convinced he had died of loneliness. She told me he never complained about being on his own but it was obvious to her he was extremely lonely without the woman he had been married to for fifty-six years. Not even a single year had passed since Grandma died. He would now join her, taking his place at her side. The more I thought of Kerry's explanation of why he died, the more it made sense. "I heard a person could die from loneliness, especially someone who had been married for so many years."

The next day, a devastating fire burned Arlington racetrack to the ground. Incredibly, not a single fatality resulted from the consuming inferno. The irony of this event was inescapable. It was clearly a sign that the end of an era had come to an abrupt close. It almost seemed fitting that the racetrack he had enjoyed for so many years was now at rest with him. Despite knowing he had led a full life, his death still saddened me beyond words. His approach to life inspired me to be like him, even though I knew I could never measure up to his greatness. He exemplified just about everything that was right in the world.

His funeral was similar to my grandmother's in that a huge contingency of family and friends were there to pay their last respects. I kept beating myself up for failing to give him more of my time. The world was definitely a different place without him. In time, I realized if I wanted to be close to him, all I had to do was think of one of the many fond memories I shared with him in the garden or at the cemetery. With the passing of my grand-parents, I was becoming acquainted with how death impacts life. Death and time are similar in that they stop or slow down for no one or nothing. Change is the essence of life, but when change is brought about by death, we are almost always caught off guard, carrying on as if things are perpetually unchangeable. I felt foolish for taking him for granted. I vowed right then and there to always put family first.

Pilgrimages to Hanover

My daughter Mallory was born the following year in 1986. I was learning how birth and death have something in common. They both bring about great change. Caring for a second child brought more responsibility, but it also brought great joy in that I now had a son and a daughter. What more could a father hope for? My recent experience with loss equipped me with a newfound appreciation for family. When I looked at my young children, I realized how their lives brought renewal in the wake of my grandparents' deaths.

John and I began making regular pilgrimages to Hanover with the purpose of visiting our diabetic sisters and giving them some time with my kids. Kerry and my mom enjoyed seeing Tyler and Mallory as well. Kerry's children were getting bigger now, and they had just started school. I think she enjoyed reliving the experience of having little ones around again. Mallory was just a baby, so she attracted plenty of attention. Tyler was a rambunctious toddler. He had a ton of personality, which he leveraged to its maximum worth. Kerry fell for it like a sack of potatoes. This was proven by the ease at which she surrendered her cupboards to him, where inside a veritable goldmine of snacks was housed. She loved watching him go through her stockpile until he finally selected something that caught his fancy. This scene was played out numerous times, but neither of them seemed to tire of it.

For Eydie and Sara, these visits became vital to their psychological health. It was one of the few things they had to look forward to. Since it was impossible for my mom and my two diabetic sisters to come to us, John and I made frequent visits to Hanover to break up their mundane living patterns. Very little had changed since I had left home. They were still hopelessly stuck in Hanover with no way out. Thinking back on it, these visits were vital to me as well. Spending time with Eydie and Sara helped me feel a little bit better about being unable to free them from their prison. I especially enjoyed watching them with my children. It felt so good to see them together.

By the time 1987 rolled around, complications from Eydie's diabetes began to pile up. Her eyesight had been slowly deteriorating over the last two years and she was fully blind. She also developed several sores on her legs that refused to heal. This left her restricted to a wheelchair. Despite these setbacks, her spirit remained intact. Whenever I brought Tyler and Mallory down to visit, she would perk up, insisting she hold both of them.

Tyler started asking a lot of questions, especially about Eydie. I tried to answer his questions, but judging by the look on his face he wasn't entirely sure of my explanations. He wanted to know if she really couldn't see. He also thought she was very lucky to have a wheelchair to get around in. I told him, "I promise you she would gladly exchange her wheelchair for a good set of legs." Tyler's comprehension of Eydie's side effects really didn't matter. The important thing was my sisters and children were spending time together. The visits were therapeutic. Whether it was Kerry's kids or mine, whenever my sisters were around their nieces and nephews, it was impossible to hide their joy.

Now at the time, Tyler was just turning two, but despite his young age he was already speaking full sentences. He was also smart enough to figure out he had two very sick aunts who dealt with a host of complications. Even to him, the seriousness of Eydie's condition was evident. Sara's appearance was less obvious, but he knew she suffered from the same affliction. In actuality, Sara was dealing with just as many problems as Eydie; they were just different problems. Sara's issues were both physical and mental. She was dealing with violent insulin reactions brought about by an inability to stabilize her diet. Worse yet were her bouts of depression that stemmed from being trapped in Hanover. She wore her sadness on her face, and it tore me apart each time I saw her.

Sara's mental ailments easily overshadowed her physical condition. After she graduated from high school, she was forced to accept the fact that having a life of her own was impossible. This realization crushed her spirit. It made me feel guilty about my own freedom and good health.

Now that I had a growing family to look after, it became harder and harder to find time for her. When I did come down, I often took her for a drive in my car. She looked forward to these temporary escapes from her dark prison, as she had come to view it. Our drives usually started out with her venting about the doldrums of being confined to Hanover. I would listen to her frustrations, consoling her whenever I could. Sara still dreamed of a quasi-normal life far removed from her current existence. Unable to offer her a way out, I did my best to play the role of the sympathizer. I couldn't help but feel the irreversible nature of her plight. It still saddens me to think of it.

As a diversionary tactic, I attempted to use my sense of humor to change the subject. I'd share with her the latest comedy material that John and I had worked on for his act. This usually proved very effective. On one such occasion I distinctly recall telling her a joke I had recently come up with concerning our father's lust for the beer can. John liked the joke so much he immediately incorporated it into his act. He sets up the joke while speaking about dreams. After sharing several of his own, he reveals his father's lifelong dream. It went something like this, "My father's lifelong dream, his lifelong dream, is to have the winning raffle ticket where the grand prize is an empty shopping cart and two minutes at Louie's Liquor Store." The first time she heard it she laughed uncontrollably. Laughter was one of the few temporary remedies to her terminal predicament.

We had several memorable drives together, but one in particular stands out. It involved a dream she had about our grandfather shortly after his passing. Intrigued, I wanted to hear everything about it. She told me the dream took place in downtown Hanover while she was running a routine errand for my mom. Partway through her excursion she stopped dead in her tracks at the sight before her. It was my grandfather; except by her estimation, he was fifty feet tall! Startled by his appearance, she said nothing. Instead, he asked her a question in his usual deep voice, "How's the baby?" Shaking her head Sara replied, "What baby?" He then said, "Why, Jim's baby." When she told him he was fine, Grandpa shook his head in approval and then disappeared.

I must confess I was a bit spellbound after Sara told me her dream. The symbolism was inescapable. The first thing that stuck in my mind was his immense size. This made perfect sense, for he was truly a giant in stature. The second and more prominent thing was that the intent of his concern was for Tyler. When I passed him that day on the highway it never dawned on me that not only had I been denied of seeing him one last time but he had also been denied of seeing his great-grandson as well. A warm feeling rushed over my body. The spiritual ramifications of this dream were unmistakable. Having read the Bible, I knew that God often used dreams to communicate with the worthy. Sara was certainly worthy of such a gift. We were convinced God permitted our grandfather one last visit from the great beyond. The revelation of her dream had taken a great deal of the sting out of his death. It also helped me to reconcile my failure of not making more time for him.

Eydie's Death

Later that year winter arrived on schedule, and with it Eydie's condition worsened. In early December things came to a head when she was urgently rushed to the hospital in Dubuque. My brother and I received a troubling call from my sister Kerry. Kerry was unsure as to the extent of what was wrong, but she made it quite clear that things were serious.

Upon receiving the news we immediately drove to the hospital to be with Eydie. We arrived just after our parents. They informed us she was being put in the Intensive Care Unit. When I saw my mother, our eyes locked. I could see the desperation on her face. Without her saying a word I knew the situation was extremely serious. It was quite some time before the doctor finally came out. He informed us that she had slipped into a diabetic coma and her chances of coming out of it were slim to none. As these words rolled off his tongue, I got that same sick-to-my-stomach feeling when I first heard the news of my grandfather.

Several days went by as she continued to hang on through artificial life support. Everyone was certain that this was it. I refused to give up hope. She had beaten the odds before, why should now be any different? I thought back to when she had received her kidney. It was still working with few signs of wear. I then thought of my grandparents, lying prostrate, giving praise to the Almighty for delivering her out of the hands of death. Perhaps God would grant her one more miracle. I prayed to God begging him to save her.

December 21 rolled around. Christmas was just a few days away. I clung to the hope that the magic of Christmas could save her. That day, everyone was summoned to the hospital as the doctors were convinced the end was near. I held tight that something miraculous could still happen. I kept searching for positives.

When I could find none, I went to her room, held her hand, and desperately pleaded for God to hear my prayers. Surely if there was ever a soul worth saving, it was Eydie's.

We continued to endure the long wait, but there would be no miracle this time. Eydie died four days before Christmas. It was the worst Christmas I ever had. Those crappy Christmases I recall so vividly from my childhood now seemed marvelous compared to this. I didn't know it then, but I sure knew it now. I was rich beyond my wildest dreams, for we had each other. I never thought I'd find myself longing for those days.

Just like my grandfather, I never saw it coming until it was too late. Once again, I would be haunted by the guilt of not taking time out of my selfish life for her. After my grandfather had passed, I told myself, "Stay near to those you are closest to by visiting often. Make sure to take time for those who are sick." I was being tortured by my own words. The little girl with the red velvety hair whose bravery I had admired for so long was now gone.

Her death devastated the entire family. There is little doubt she went directly to heaven. Her courageous approach in the face of overwhelming odds was exceeded only by her steadfast faith. She never once complained or cursed her Creator for the hand she had been dealt. She was an inspiration to all who knew her. It was her faith that truly defined her. We mourned her for the terrible suffering she withstood throughout her life. I kept trying to make sense of it all. I told myself, "Why should someone so pure, so genuine, be given such a life as hers?" Everyone cried, even my father. She deserved better.

My limited understanding of God's purpose made it easy for me to affix blame to him. After all, he had the power to save if he wanted to. He could have easily saved her from all of it. What I failed to recognize at that time in my life is that he did save her. He saved her from a long life of suffering by taking her to a place he had prepared for her. Now my faith was being put to the test … and I wasn't doing very well.

The irony of a Christmas funeral requires little explanation. Christmas was supposed to be a time of giving and receiving, not taking. There was no Christmas spirit, only despair. I kept thinking of my mother, who now had to deal with the loss of a child as well as one of her closest companions. I thought, *What greater pain is there than the death of your own child?* Having children of my own, I tried not to imagine what that must have felt like.

After the funeral I returned home to share some quiet moments with my mother. Despite the intense suffering she had endured, her motherly instincts were still sharp enough to reveal my tormented soul. She told me to stop beating myself up over her death. She told me to take comfort in knowing that Eydie was in a far better place and finally free from her pain. She reminded me of the special relationship she had with Grandma and how they were now reunited in heaven. She also mentioned how much Eydie loved my children. She knew who they were. What a wondrous gift that was. I slowly digested her words. She was so right. Without speaking a word, I gave her an agreeing nod. My mother made me realize it had nothing to do with my selfish needs or my misguided prayers. It was about Eydie. She had given her all and crossed the finish line in triumphant fashion.

The first couple of months of life without Eydie were a bit rough. My brother and I spoke of her often, vowing to each other we would always keep her memory alive. My father actually summed her up best. He described her as a fierce woman, very fierce. Aptly put, for she led her life courageously fearing nothing but God. She was a lot like Grandma. It's no wonder my grandmother was drawn to her. In the later part of her life she was the only person who could stand up to my father without any retaliation. Whenever she laid into him, he remained silent until her tongue-lashing was over. He would often let out a chuckle once she was through. Other than my grandmother, no one else dared to put him in his place. Never was there a more beautiful life. I missed her terribly and still do.

Death of John and Sara

In the spring of 1988, I made the decision to move my family to Florida. I had previously spent a couple of winters working at the greyhound park in Hollywood, Florida. I had gained the favor of the general manager of the track, George Eckert, who told me if I ever moved to Florida there would always be a job waiting for me. After weighing my options I decided to accept his offer, believing it to be the best course of action to improve the life of my family. I was certain if things were going to get better, I had to leave Dubuque.

Now that Eydie's suffering was over, the rest of the family appeared to be in good shape, at least from a health standpoint. Sara was still a concern, but she was excited for me, despite the fact that we would be separated by a thousand miles.

Shortly after I left, my brother John was diagnosed with leukemia and died in less than two years. His death ravaged my soul. It was the absolute low point in my life, or at least I thought it was.

When I had returned home for his funeral, I was informed by my mother that Sara had been taken to the hospital for what was described as diabetic dementia. Concerned, I promised my mother I would visit her before leaving. With the death of my brother still fresh in my mind, I grossly underestimated the seriousness of Sara's condition. I wrote off her sudden illness as merely her way of dealing with John's death.

When I spoke to my mother about Sara, she believed her setback had been slowly building from Eydie's death. It had now gone full blown with John's passing. She said her blood sugar levels had been haywire for quite some time. The culprit was her diet. Her depression had led to unhealthy eating habits. I shook my head and wondered, *Is there ever any good news?*

When I arrived at her room at the hospital, I saw her propped up in bed in much the same manner as my grandmother had been when I visited her shortly before her death. Just like Grandma, she was staring off into space. At first, she never even saw me, or at least she didn't register my presence. When I got closer, her eyes opened like saucers, she opened up her arms, called out my name, and immediately began crying.

At first I thought her tears were tears of happiness to see me and, of course, the sadness that John's death had brought, but when we embraced, she put a bear hug on me that no force in all of nature could have broken. I couldn't help but sense there was more to her setback than just recent events. I attempted to put her at ease by telling her everything was going to be okay. I told her she had to be brave like John and strong like Eydie. I told her not to worry about anything except getting better. I told her she needed to get better so we could spend some time together the next time I returned home. There was an emptiness to her listening. I was very worried.

I did most of the talking after this, reassuring her she still had a brother, sister, and mother who loved her. I still couldn't help feel it was going in one ear and out the other. I had never seen her so tired. I kissed her forehead and told her goodbye. Although I was greatly concerned for her well-being, I never thought for a second that this moment would be our last.

Over the next month, each time I called my mother, she gave me an update on Sara's condition. My mother never once suspected Sara's life was in danger. I know this because my mom always said she thought Sara was improving and believed she would be coming home soon. But there would be no homecoming. On June 24, 1990, just a little over a month since my brother John had died of cancer, my sister Kerry called to tell me Sara had passed away. Upon hearing the news my body literally crumpled in shock. I remember crying out the words, "No! Not Sara!"

My parents had now lost their third child, and I had lost my third sibling. I no longer knew how to console my mother. Every time I called her we did more crying than talking. The world seemed so empty. I hadn't even finished grieving over John's death, and now I had to deal with losing Sara as well. I didn't want to tell myself I had hit rock bottom for fear something else might happen. Far away and emotionally and financially broken, I couldn't even afford a plane ticket home to attend her funeral. I'm not sure which was worse, the grief or the guilt for not being able to pay my last respects to her.

For the fifth time in my life, someone close to me died without me being able to fully see it coming. I had failed Sara just like I had failed John, Eydie, and my grandparents. Of all the deaths I had experienced to that point, none was more painful than Sara's. Seeing her propped up like Grandma was a foreshadowing of things to come, and when she hugged me so tightly, I should have known right then and there that something was terribly wrong. It was her way of making a desperate cry for help, but I missed it, just like I had missed so many other signals from those who needed me most. I was the big brother who was supposed to have looked out for his little sister. Guilt of an unimaginable magnitude began to set in.

A Flower in the Desert

I was in utter ruins. My heart was being bombarded by unrelenting waves of sorrow. I believed with all of my being I had literally let down just about everyone who ever needed me in my life. I digressed into an emotionless, living zombie, haunted daily by my failure-filled past. My desolation was complete. Initially, I tried to put the blame on God. I struggled with that notion until time convinced me it was my lack of action that prompted God into forsaking me. Overcome by grief, I believed I was destined to be a miserable soul living a miserable life. I was certain my selfish nature was to blame. It was my penance for failing to act when my loved ones needed me most.

I was literally teetering on a fine line between sanity and a complete mental breakdown. The slightest nudge by no more than a fingertip could have easily sent me over the edge. Just when it looked like I had reached the point of no return, a miracle took place. Out of the blue, I received a phone call from John's daughter, Sarah. Sarah was twelve years old. She told me her family was moving to Florida. Even more incredible, they were going to be living less than a half hour away from where I lived! The timing of this was nothing short of miraculous. Talk about saving grace! Sarah's arrival to Florida was like an epiphany. It instantaneously dislodged me from the pit of guilt in which I had become so hopelessly entrenched. Her arrival to Florida gave me a higher calling. She was the one person for me, and I was the one person for her who could bring healing to our broken hearts. Who would have thought a little girl could have brought me back from the depths of depression? It was as if she had been sent special delivery from 3,000 miles away just so we could get our lives back on track. The Lord sure does work in mysterious ways.

After speaking with Debbie, Sarah's mother, she was gracious in allowing me and my children to visit Sarah on a regular basis. She also let me have her for an occasional day trip. I continued to see Sarah on a regular basis. We didn't speak much of John. I decided if she had questions about her father I would answer, but I didn't want to risk upsetting her further. For me, the comfort of her company was all I needed. She brightened my world each time I saw her. Seeing her with my children was even more gratifying. Sarah and Mallory made a strong connection. It soothed my soul to see them together. We continued our visits with Sarah for the next year and half until her family moved back to California. Her departure was like a flare going off, signaling it was time for me to leave Florida as well. I soon became obsessed with the idea that I had to get out of Florida. Florida had become a constant reminder of the terrible things that had recently gone wrong in my life. I didn't know how, but I knew I had to get out. Ironically, shortly after Sarah left, the opportunity presented itself.

About a year before Sarah left, I traded in my dog-racing career for a more stable life. I accepted a position with a specialty retailer called the Honey Baked Ham Company. By the fall of 1991, the break I was looking for finally came. I learned that the company was looking for managers to help open a store in Tennessee. It wasn't exactly what I had in mind, but at this point, anything was better than Florida. I immediately applied for the position, and within a couple of weeks, I had the job. I'm sure for most people leaving Florida for Tennessee wouldn't even be remotely enticing, but I could not have been more relieved to go. Something inside kept telling me it was the only way I could get on with my life. So, in the fall of 1991, I moved my family to Nashville, Tennessee, hoping that a change of scenery would help me put my dark past to rest.

Life after Death

It's well known that when a person experiences a death, they go through five distinct stages of grief. The five stages are denial, anger, bargaining, depression, and acceptance. I can attest to going through each of these. I would also like to add one more to the list: God abandonment.

Before ever leaving Florida I had ceased going to church. I can't say I ever fully stopped believing in God, I just came to the conclusion I had shamed him to the point that I was of little significance to him. Therefore, I abandoned God, for I was certain he had abandoned me. However, I did keep the promise I made when my children were baptized. That promise was to raise them in the faith. So every Sunday I dropped them off at a nearby Methodist church where they attended Sunday school on a regular basis.

When I accepted the job transfer to Nashville, I hoped the change of scenery would heal my tragic past. Initially it worked.

Between the move and starting a new job, I found little time to drown in my sorrows. Unfortunately, this didn't last long. Once I had settled in, those devastating feelings of guilt, loss, and hurt came rushing back with a vengeance. It seemed like the harder I tried to block out the deaths the worse it got. I kept asking myself, "Why has God abandoned me? What on earth did I do to deserve such grief?" I knew I had failed him just like I did my family. Regardless of the reasons, I felt lost, with little or no purpose to my life.

I can scarcely describe the level of anger I was dealing with at this time. When looking back at my life in retrospection, I saw nothing more than thirty years of agonizing events. I had searched and searched for answers, but found none. I had now digressed into a resentful person, believing I had been personally jaded by God. My narrow-minded beliefs held him personally responsible for everything that had gone wrong in my life. I concluded that for whatever reason, I was destined to be a miserable soul trapped in a miserable life.

An Earthly Angel

Shortly after I had turned from God, a sequence of events began to unfold that ultimately changed my life forever. It all began on a Sunday morning when I was going through the routine of dropping my children off at church for Sunday school. I had returned to pick them up, but I was a bit early, so I stepped out of my vehicle and leaned back against the fender of my car while I waited for them to come out.

It was a very peaceful morning, the sun was shining brightly, and the birds were singing loudly. As I relaxed a bit more, I couldn't help but take notice of the architectural design of the church. Towering twin steeples pointed skyward like two enormous arms reaching toward heaven. The outside of the church was painted pure white. It was highlighted by several sets of beautiful stained glass windows. As I continued to marvel at this profound structure, I found myself wondering how many people had come through its doors seeking refuge from the cold hard world. Just then, the church bells began to chime, and as they did, out of the corner of my eye I detected a figure standing right next to me that seemed to have appeared out of nowhere. Startled, I jumped back. Standing right next to me was a woman who looked to be in her early fifties. She was dressed in white from head to toe. This is no exaggeration. She wore white shoes, white stockings, a white dress, and a white hat, and all of her attire was as brilliant as a fresh snow. She had a confident ear-to-ear smile that was accentuated by a pair of rosy cheeks and piercing eyes. For a moment, I thought she might be an angel. In time I would come to learn that she was an earthly angel, heaven sent to free me from my pain.

She spoke softly, but her words were penetrating. Calmly she said, "I've noticed you before waiting to pick up your children. I heard you have suffered through much loss and thought you might be interested in coming to a class I teach on Wednesday nights. It's primarily for people who've been divorced, but anyone who has endured loss is welcome to come." She went on to say, "For many, divorce is like a death. Sometimes just listening to those who've been through similar experiences can bring a new perspective." She then told me how to find the room and said, "If you'd like to come, be there at eight o'clock sharp." I thanked her for the invite, but inside I had no intention of going.

The following day I had pretty much shrugged off the incident with the lady in white. Still finding it hard to sleep at night, I spent many evenings watching endless hours of television, which effectively turned my brain into a gelatinous blob. My spirit became equally numbed. In this television-induced vegetative state, I managed to temporarily escape my past. Within a relatively short time, I became a "full-blown channel-surfing addict." I fell into a routine where each night after work I'd come home, spend a little time with the kids, and then do my best Jekyll and Hyde impersonation by transforming myself into a "television zombie." During my many hours of channel surfing, I kept running across a television commercial that zealously proclaimed God's love for all of mankind. I soon became agitated by the frequency at which it appeared. One night, after seeing it appear countless times, I decided to put a swift end to this annoying intrusion by turning off the television and going to bed.

The next day was an off day from work. Out of spite, I eliminated any possibility for the commercial to reappear by simply leaving the television off. I quickly concocted a new strategy to avoid God: I would get lost in a good book. This would leave no room for godly intrusions, or at least so I thought.

Within a very short time the peacefulness I had been enjoying became shattered by the sound of my clamoring doorbell. When I jumped up to open the door, I found two gentlemen in white shirts and black ties standing at the entrance. They were Jehovah's Witnesses. Before I could say a word, one of them shouted out loudly saying, "Do you have Jesus in your life?" Now, I wanted to say, "I did, but he rejected me." Fortunately, common sense told me not to open that can of worms. So, instead, I told them I was a member of the United Methodist faith. To my surprise, they were genuinely happy for me. In fact, they were so happy they began to pray for me. They prayed I would always stay close to God and never doubt his love for me. I thought, *If they only knew!*

By now, I was more than just mildly agitated by these spiritual intrusions. Determined more than ever to rid myself of godly influences, I placed my book down, put on some tennis shoes, and literally started running from God. I confidently told myself, "Now let's see him try to persuade me!" The subdivision I lived in was located on the edge of town. Beyond its perimeter was nothing but countryside. I took off in the direction of this wilderness. I ran down my street as hard as I could for more than a mile until I found myself surrounded by nature. I kept running until I couldn't run anymore. Finally, out of breath, I hunched over, gasping for air with both of my hands resting on my knees. When I finally began to regain my breath, I slowly lifted my head up. I glanced across an open field where my eyes became fixed on a nearby hill that overlooked an interstate highway. There, situated on the very top of the hill, was an enormous billboard. The background of the billboard was completely black while the inscription contained only two words in bold white print that simply said, "He lives." Moved beyond belief, I said to myself, "Even when I run from God, he still finds me!" I looked toward heaven and surrendered right there. At the top of my lungs I cried out, "Okay, God, you win! Let me do whatever it is you would have me do!" I wasn't remotely sure of what that was, but I was certain God was trying to tell me something.

The next day came and this experience, as well as the encounter with the woman in white, increasingly gnawed at me. No matter how hard I tried, I couldn't resist connecting the dots. I believed God was urging me to accept the offer from the woman in white. Despite feeling apprehensive with the whole idea, something inside kept urging me to find out what this was all about.

Wednesday finally arrived. Thoughts of changing my mind about attending the class kept resurfacing all day long. I fought off these doubts with the rationale that I'd drive myself crazy if I didn't go. I continued to wait for eight o'clock to come. It seemed like the longest day of my life. Finally the time drew near. I looked up at the clock. It was ten minutes to eight and time to go. I hopped in my car still wondering what on earth I was doing.

I arrived at the church a few minutes before eight. I found myself at the door of the class. It was open. I could hear voices from outside the door. Upon entering I noticed several small groups of people engaged in conversation. A look around the room revealed wooden floors and a podium at the far end of the room surrounded by a dozen or so chairs. Other than these few fixtures the room was essentially bare, with the exception of a familiar painting of the Savior that I recognized from my childhood. I soon made eye contact with my angel, who promptly greeted me. She expressed how happy she was that I had come. We chatted for a few seconds and then everyone took a seat.

Before commencing, my angel said a short prayer thanking God for allowing us to have this time together. Since I was the newcomer, she took a moment to introduce me to the group. She explained to them that I was not divorced but nevertheless had suffered through much loss in my life. To say the least it felt a little awkward having these strangers stare at me. I couldn't help but wonder what they were thinking.

After exchanging salutations with the group, she introduced a lady who had volunteered to give a testimony concerning her recent struggles. She was a woman in her early forties who was visibly shaking as she made her way toward the podium. I assumed she was nervous, but I sensed something more than nerves. I wasn't quite sure what to make of this, but I was strangely intrigued by her fragility.

When she approached the podium, her quivering became even more pronounced. Her voice trembled as she spoke. She began her story by telling the group that shortly after she had graduated from high school, she married a man of considerable wealth. They stayed married for twenty happy years. During those years she wanted for nothing. In fact, she had it all: a big house, a three-car garage, a swimming pool, and every other creature comfort known to mankind.

The trouble started when their only child, a sixteen-year-old daughter, wanted to go to a party that many of her friends were attending. At the time, she had only been driving for less than a year. A disagreement broke out between Mom and Dad as to whether she should be allowed to go. Dad said no, Mom said yes. Mom ultimately won out, so their daughter left for the party. Later that evening she was killed in an automobile accident. Devastated by the tragic event, her husband blamed her for the death of their daughter. Soon after, he filed for a divorce.

She went on to tell the group about the prenuptial agreement she had signed when she married her husband. In a matter of days she went from extremely comfortable to nearly destitute. Though it was clear what really hurt the most was the dissolution of her family. She felt forever separated by her loss, a feeling with which I was all too familiar. Being on the outside looking in, her story offered me a bird's-eye view of seeing someone other than myself dealing with horrific loss. It was extremely humbling.

The story didn't end there. She went on to tell the group how she was living in a one-bedroom efficiency apartment working as a waitress at a local diner. She had no car or phone, which sounded hauntingly familiar. She was an only child with no extended family, or in other words, completely alone. She did, however, have one thing, an unbreakable faith in God above. She was certain God would bring her deliverance. She finished her testimony by reminding us that with God, *all* things are possible.

As I sat there listening to her story, I became ashamed of how I had dealt with my loss. Here was someone who was far worse off than I had ever been. At least I had a decent job, a solid roof over my head, and family who loved me. I was practically rich in comparison to this woman. It was a definite wake-up call that made me realize just how blessed I was. If only I could have been half as courageous as this woman. She had literally lost everything, yet her trust in God above remained firmly intact. Witnessing such faith had a pronounced effect on me.

This experience marked the turning point in my struggle to accept what had happened. I viewed this event as a revelation from God. In one massive swoop he had saved me from myself by allowing me to witness someone else's faith being put to a far more difficult test than my own. This woman's testimony had opened my eyes to everything I had gone through. In that moment I realized it was never about me. The destiny of my loved ones had nothing to do with my selfish feelings. I was never cheated, but instead, blessed by the time I had shared with them. This is why I have always believed I was chosen. I don't say that boastingly, for surely I would be the first to admit I am not deserving of such a gift, but I was sure of one thing. I had been saved by grace and grace alone. I realized I could never give up on God again. From that point forward, my outlook on life drastically changed. I realized God had been there for me the entire time. I, on the other hand, had been doing everything in my power to ignore his outstretched hands, which included a childish display of running away from him.

When it was all said and done, I thanked the woman and my angel for helping me to see the light. We prayed together and gave thanks to God. Soon thereafter I started attending church again on a regular basis. My angel also taught a Sunday morning class for adults, which I regularly attended until I was asked to teach a children's class. I accepted the offer. I found that teaching children was especially healing. I discovered their faith was stronger than my own. My renewal was almost complete. I vowed never again to lose faith regardless of how bad things got. I was ready to live again.

Homecoming

Moving to Nashville turned out to be the best thing that ever happened to me. I was finally looking forward to each day. It was true. Life does go on, but not without the self-realization that my loved ones who preceded me in death are merely waiting for me to join them in paradise. Good coming from bad never felt so good.

Coming to Nashville not only salvaged my soul but offered me another huge comfort. I could go home. Hanover was only twelve hours away. I'd have to wait until the following summer to go back home to visit, but it gave me something to look forward to. When the summer of 1992 finally rolled around, I took a week of vacation and headed back home for my first real homecoming in nearly four years. I brought my children with me. I knew they could lift my mom's spirit in a way that I could not. I vividly remember our reunion as if it were yesterday. It was late in the afternoon on a Saturday when we pulled up in front of the old house. My father's van was nowhere in sight, so I assumed he was either at the garden or in the tavern. I was taken back when I laid eyes on the tiny house I used to call home. It hadn't changed one bit, with the exception of a little more wear and tear since I'd last seen it. The front door was open. I walked up to the outside glass door and peered into the kitchen. There was my mom, patiently waiting for me. She had not detected my presence. When she did see me, she ran to the door with open arms. Our bear hug embrace was much more than a long-awaited reunion; an unspoken release from the sorrows of our past took place without a word being said.

When I laid eyes on my mom, I was surprised to see how much she had aged. I hadn't seen her since John's funeral. Whenever we spoke on the phone her voice always sounded the same, never once giving me any indication of the physical changes I saw before me. The deaths had aged us all, but it took an especially heavy toll on her. She had gone completely gray. Her face resembled an old Navaho Indian woman who had spent too many years roaming about the desert in search of answers. She was sixty-one years old.

Looking on her face made my heart heavy. It was obvious that each time one of her children died, a little of her died too. She was especially devastated by the loss of the two girls. She had been Sara and Eydie's primary caregiver for almost thirty years. Their deaths created a void in her life that could never be filled. I felt so sad for her. The majority of her life had been one of disappointment and tragic loss. It seemed so unfair. She had her shortcomings, but don't we all? She had given everything to her children, especially Eydie and Sara, yet she remained a prisoner of guilt, believing she should have done more. I could scarcely imagine what she must have gone through after they died. My father seldom spoke of their deaths; it was his way. Unfortunately, this only added to my mother's loneliness.

I spent quite a few hours consoling my mom during that first visit. I told her of my anger with God and my misguided resentment toward him. Then I told her how he had brought me back to the fold. She took comfort in my spiritual renewal. We talked about the afterlife, wondering what it must be like for them. I assured her they were looking down on us. I told her they were the ones who should feel bad. After all, they were in paradise while we were still stuck here. She agreed by shaking her head and letting out a little chuckle. It felt good to see her laugh.

She was overjoyed to see Tyler and Mallory again. Tyler was seven years old and Mallory was five. When they hugged, a glow came over her face. It didn't last long, but it was a glimpse of happier times from long ago. It's good to know that some things never change.

Even though I had a pretty good idea of where my father was, I had to ask my mother about him. She confirmed my suspicions of him being at the tavern. She told me she didn't have a clue as to when he'd be coming home. She went on to tell me he was ornery as ever and could still drink and chew with the best of them. It's sad to know that some things never change.

A few moments later he pulled up in front of the house in his van. He no longer had the old van that was indelibly engraved in my mind. He had replaced it with a newer model. It was still a Ford, but this one was exceptionally repulsive, and not just because he had torn out the seats like its predecessor. The big difference was the color. It was powder puff blue, which seemed hardly befitting to his Darth Vader image.

He eventually got around to stepping out of his van. When he did, my eyes nearly flew out of their sockets. He was enormous. He looked more like Jabba the Hutt than Darth Vader. He easily weighed more than three hundred pounds! His gut was so distended that he was unable to see his own shoes when standing. His face was just as beet red as it was the day he taught me how to tie my shoes, except this time it wasn't from anger, it was from a lack of oxygen.

Walking through the door he spotted my kids and began calling out to them. He said, "Come over here and give your grandpa a big kiss!" I'll never forget my daughter looking up at me with frightened eyes quietly pleading, "Do we have to, Dad?" I couldn't deny him. He was still their grandfather, and he hadn't seen them in years. I told them to go see their grandfather.

He wasn't fully tanked but you could tell he had a few in him. He also had a few noticeable chew deposits clinging to the corner of his mouth. He hugged and kissed Tyler first. I guess Tyler figured that by going first he'd get it over with. After the deed was done, I noticed a big dollop of chew adhered to Tyler's cheek. I couldn't help but notice the close resemblance he made to "John-boy Walton." Mallory was next. She let out a few small whimpers when he raked his whiskers across her smooth cheeks. She couldn't wait for it to be over. When he was finished with Mallory he came over to me as well. I guess I deserved the same treatment for subjecting my kids to it. I could smell the foul stench of alcohol on his breath. It repulsed me and brought back dark flashbacks from my childhood.

While in Hanover, I spent some evenings trying to look up old friends. I wasn't sure who was still around and who had left, but I learned the local bars held most of the clues. While making the rounds, I ran into some familiar faces. I even bumped into a few old friends from school who were able to make a go of it in Hanover. They pretty much told me who had left and who was still around. When we finished, I headed back to Kerry's house, or should I say my grandparents' house? To me, it will always be my grandparents' house. Don't get me wrong, I was happy Kerry and her family were living in the house. I couldn't imagine anyone else living there, but I will always think of the house as my grandparents', and in spite of their departure from this world, I still find myself giving thanks to them for showing me the spiritual way to lead my life.

It was after midnight when I turned the corner to my old street. I noticed a light still on at my parents' house. I decided to stop over to see if my mom was still up. The door was unlocked. I stepped inside and immediately recognized the sound of my father snoring loudly. He was laying in the same old worn-out cot I so vividly recalled from my childhood. I could see a light on in my sister's bedroom. I saw my mom lying on Eydie's bed reading a book. I made a little noise to alert her to my presence. She put down her book when I entered the room. She asked me if I had a good time. I told her yes, but more importantly I asked, "Why are you still up?" She replied, "Since the two girls died, I haven't had a good night's sleep in years." She had been routinely sleeping in the girl's room for quite some time. It was as close as she could be to them now. I told her I had encountered many sleepless nights myself. Whenever my mom anguished over her daughters, I tried my best to soothe her pain. I reassured her they were in a far better place now. She believed this; she just missed them terribly.

The girls' beds were just as they had always been, pushed together side by side. I sat down next to my mom on Sara's bed. My sisters' room was still arranged in the exact same way as it had been when I lived at home. The old dresser and the two beds were still the only furnishings in the room. My choice was either to sit down on Sara's bed or sit down on the floor. I chose the bed. We chatted about old times for a good hour or so before I started getting tired. My mom told me that if I wanted, I could sleep next to her in Sara's bed. It seemed a little weird at first, but I knew there was no way I could tell her no. I sensed she wanted me to stay with her. I figured if it made her happy, I should do it.

That night I had an incredible dream. I dreamt I was in my home with my two sisters. To my bewilderment, my sisters were completely free from all of their sicknesses. They had a glow about them, the same way my brother looked when I had the dream of him a couple of years before. Unlike the dream I had of my brother, I never woke up from this dream until the morning. There wasn't any speaking in this dream either. The fact nothing was said was unimportant, for the revelation was the miracle of their restored health. I thanked God for letting me see them completely healthy for the first time. Just like the dream with John, I felt certain they were okay.

I remember waking up the next morning feeling exceptionally rejuvenated. I couldn't wait to tell my mother about the dream I had. Before I could begin to tell her about my dream, she told me she had the best night's sleep in years. She looked incredibly refreshed. She continued to carry on about her restful night. She couldn't get over how soundly she had slept. This was turning out to be as big of a miracle as my dream. Anxiously I waited for her to finish so I could tell her about my dream. When I did, a huge smile came over her face. My dream seemed to ease her troubled conscience.

From that year forward I returned home each summer to visit. The summer of 1994 turned out to be an eventful one. I earned a big promotion at work. For the first time I would run a store of my own in St. Louis, Missouri. I was to begin managing it in the fall. I was ecstatic over this opportunity for a couple of reasons. St. Louis was less than six hours from home. This meant I could get back and forth to home over a weekend, if necessary. My mom's health had begun to decline over the past year, so being closer could not have come at a more opportune time. Ironically, she had been diagnosed with type II diabetes. She was also dealing with high blood pressure and poor circulation. Moving to St. Louis would be a huge boost for me personally as well as professionally, and although I remained greatly concerned for my mother's well-being, at least I was closer now.

Before leaving Nashville my kids and I made our summer pilgrimage to Hanover. My mom was ecstatic over my promotion and relocation to St. Louis. Although she was a dedicated Chicago Cubs fan, she had always admired the winning tradition of the St.

Louis Cardinals. She also had a long-term infatuation with Cardinal great, Stan Musial. She always said that if he ever asked her to marry him, she'd drop the old man in a heartbeat. Too bad Stan never made it to Hanover.

You Never Know What It's Doing at the Ball Park

During our time in Hanover I had promised Tyler I would take him to a Cubs game. He was well aware of the many excursions my brother and I had made to Wrigley Field in the past. He was extremely excited to leave his mark on the tradition. I hadn't been to a Cubs game in more than five years, so I guess you could say I had the itch too. We decided to go in on a Friday. The Cubs would be taking on the Houston Astros in a one o'clock start.

When we awoke Friday morning we were greeted by indigo skies accompanied by a steady rain. I talked it over with my mom and she pretty much agreed that we should cancel our adventure. When Tyler got up, he was oblivious to the weather conditions. I broke it to him by telling him I wasn't about to drive four hours in the rain to a game that was almost certain to be postponed. Tyler looked up at me and said, "You never know what it's doing at the ballpark, Dad." As soon as I heard my son speak those words, a warm feeling rushed over me. It felt like a sign from heaven. I looked back at Tyler and said, "That's it. We're going!" He cheered, of course, but my mom looked befuddled at my sudden change of heart. I had never told either of them how often John had spoken those exact same words in the exact same situation years before. It was crystal clear to me, we were meant to go.

Time was becoming a factor, as it was almost nine a.m. If we were going to make it before the first pitch, we had to get going. My mom was still perplexed by my sudden change in plans. She must have thought I was crazy, but I didn't have time to explain. Tyler and I kissed her goodbye and off we went.

The drive would take a good four hours, which meant our ETA would be right around the opening pitch. After being on the road for about an hour or so, the rains gradually began to subside. A short while later the clouds started to part giving way to clear blue skies. I just shook my head, all the while sensing John's presence.

If you've ever been to Wrigley, you know that finding a parking space can be a nightmare. We didn't have tickets either, so not only was there a strong likelihood of being late, we'd most likely be sitting in either the nosebleed section or the bleachers at best. It really didn't matter much to Tyler or me. The beautiful weather we'd been given to see our first major league ball game together as a father and son was more than enough reward.

When we arrived at the ballpark, it was ten minutes before game time. I swung down the first street I found, which was one of many that formed a labyrinth around Wrigley's outfield. To my complete astonishment, the second or third parking spot on the first street I pulled onto was unoccupied. I couldn't believe it. Before pulling in, I glanced down the seemingly endless avenue. There was not one other empty parking spot to be found!

We parked in that seemingly reserved spot, locked up the car, and then ran to get in line at the first ticket booth we came to. After a short wait in line, half-kidding, I asked the ticket vendor if there was anything close to the field. To my amazement, he said there were still two seats available in the first row on the first base side. He told us the only reason these seats hadn't sold was because everyone who had inquired about them had four or more people in their group. These seats were located on Houston's side of the field, but we could have cared less. Being this close to the field was a dream I could have never imagined, especially considering our last-minute arrival. I was starting to get chills at this point. In all of our trips to Wrigley, John and I had never experienced sitting in the first row for a Cubs game!

Without the least bit of hesitation I purchased those tickets. Once they were in our hands, we were off like two kids chasing an ice cream truck. Dressed in our Cubs shirts we headed for our ringside seats. I wondered how many of the opposing teams' fans we'd see. Surprisingly, there were very few Houston fans. In fact, the section was predominately inhabited with Cubs fans. The only exception was one harmless grandfather with his two grandsons. This was too good to be true.

The weather, the parking spot, the seats, everything was going our way. If only now we could bring home a Cubs victory, then the day would be perfect. During the game there must have been at least half a dozen foul ball opportunities that came within a few feet of us. We never caught one, but Tyler and I had a blast trying to corral them. The game itself was a seesaw affair highlighted by four home runs, two by each team, including the game winner in an extra inning affair by none other than Cubs legend Mark Grace. At the start of the bottom of the eleventh inning, Mark Grace walked up to the plate. On the second or third pitch, he hit a towering drive that landed in the bleachers for a dramatic game winning home run. The "walk off" shot easily cleared the wall, sending 30,000-plus delirious fans to Cubs victory heaven.

Tyler and I were having the time of our lives. It was an incredible day. I kept thinking of John. I knew he was close. He had always wanted to take Tyler to a Cubs game. Inside I felt that dream had now been fulfilled.

After the game, Tyler and I, along with a number of other avid Cub fans, were among the last to leave. That day there was a cup promotion with illustrations of various Cubs players from the sixties. It made me think of John and the glorious wiffle ball days. Tyler found cups of all of our favorite players when John and I were kids. He collected the entire set which included Ron Santo, Ernie Banks, Billy Williams, Ferguson Jenkins, Randy Hundley, Jim Hickman, Don Kessinger, and Glenn Beckert. It was just one more sign of John's presence.

Once Tyler had finished collecting cups, I reminded him it was time to leave for we still had a four-hour trip in front of us. He looked around trying to find a reason to stay a bit longer. It didn't take him long to find one. He noticed a large group of Cub fans lining up in front of the Cubs dugout. He wanted to know what was going on. I pointed over at Mark Grace who was being interviewed on the field for his game-winning heroics. I told him once he finished his interview he'd probably sign a few autographs before exiting through the dugout. Naturally Tyler insisted that we try too. Sometimes I think I'm my own worst enemy. I rolled my eyes knowing we didn't have a snowball's chance in hell of getting his autograph. I attempted to reason with him by reminding him we were already late from the game going into extra innings, and besides, way too many kids had already beaten us to the spot. Undeterred by my hopeless assessment of the situation, he begged for us to try anyway, so, like the pushover dad that I was, we walked over and took our place in line along with the rest of the hopefuls.

While venturing over to the Cubs' dugout, we were forced to make our way to the end of the line that stretched all the way down into short left field. We were literally as far from the dugout as you could get. We stood there in the afternoon sun watching Grace finish up his interview until he slowly made his way off the field. Oddly enough, he started walking directly toward us. I leaned over to Tyler and said, "Hey, Tyler, I think he's coming this way." Tyler calmly replied, "I know, Dad." He said it like he expected Grace to come right to us. Perplexed by his confidence, I repeated myself with a little more enthusiasm this time, "Tyler, I think he's really coming over here!" Again he calmly responded, "I know, Dad." Within a few more short moments Mark Grace was standing directly in front of us signing his first post-game autograph for Tyler. I was completely flabbergasted. I began to wonder if this whole day was just a dream.

Star struck, my mind raced as I tried to think of something intelligent to say. I had it. I congratulated him on the home run he'd hit to win the game. He thanked me and said, "Maybe this will get the Cubs back on the winning track." We thanked him and said goodbye as we watched him sign a few more autographs before leaving the ballpark. I bent over and said to Tyler, "I think God just graced us with Grace."

Could things possibly get any better? We were way beyond our definition of satisfaction. We finally headed out of the ballpark. As we were leaving the friendly confines, a car happened to be pulling out from one of the VIP garages right where we were walking. We looked over at the driver and believe it or not, it was none other than Sammy Sosa! We weren't able to get his autograph, but Tyler managed to put his hand on Sammy's arm that was resting on the open window of the driver's side of his car. He smiled at us and waved before heading off. Tyler lifted his hand up in victory proclaiming he would never wash that hand again. I kept on wondering, "What else is going to happen?"

The way things were going we were surprised we made it back to our car without running into Harry Caray or some other notable personality. Talk about the ultimate father and son day! I looked toward the heavens and thanked God for giving me a memory I would treasure for the rest of my days.

About halfway into our trip back home we started to get pretty hungry. I knew I was nearly broke, but I still had a few bucks left to get us something light to snack on. From the highway I spotted a convenience store and promptly pulled off. I told Tyler we could split the last four dollars I had on me. It wouldn't buy much, but as least it would tide us over until we got home. Before I had decided on what I wanted to eat, Tyler came back to me pointing at the scratch-off lottery ticket sign. He asked me if it was okay if he could spend his two dollars on scratch-offs. I told him that was fine as long as he realized it was either food or lottery tickets. My warning didn't even make him flinch; he was determined to take his chances on the lottery tickets.

We stepped up to the counter and I purchased two one-dollar lottery tickets that he had picked out. Meanwhile, while he was scratching away, I resumed my search for something to eat, but before I could do so, my concentration became abruptly broken by the sound of Tyler's voice shouting, "Dad! Fifty bucks! Fifty bucks! I got a fifty-buck winner!" At first I thought, *Surely he's mistaken. After all, nine-year-old kids have been known to get the cart before the horse.* I casually glanced over to check the ticket. When I did, my eyes opened like saucers. He indeed had a fifty-dollar winner!

As we reveled in our newfound fortune I noticed an Illinois State Trooper standing next to Tyler. He was a distinguished-looking gentleman probably in his early fifties. When he overheard Tyler celebrating, he walked up to him and in a low, serious tone, he asked, "How old are you, son?" The officer winked at me, but Tyler looked fearful, wondering if he was being arrested for breaking the law. The trooper let out a laugh, and only then did Tyler let out a sigh of relief, realizing the officer was just having some fun with him.

We cashed in our winner and agreed that a good dinner was in order. We opted for an Italian restaurant where we enjoyed a feast.

It was the icing on the cake for what had turned out to be one of our finest days as a father and son. This was truly a day among days. I had never had a day quite like this before. We were blessed beyond repose. I couldn't stop thinking of John. Unquestionably, he had been with us the entire time.

It's Finally Over

By late summer of 1994 I had completed my move to St. Louis. Running a store completely on my own for the very first time was a big step for me. I was proud to be the captain of the ship and enjoyed the challenge of knowing I was solely responsible for the outcome of the business. This move seemed to suit me well. Inside it just felt right, like I belonged here.

The first weekend I was off, I went home to see the family. It was a big relief to know that if I needed to get home I could accomplish the journey in half a day. Reconnecting with my mom, Kerry, and her kids on a regular basis began to sew up some of the tears in the family fabric. My mom especially benefited from my visits. Each time I made the trip, I could tell it lifted her spirit. My father on the other hand was heading in the opposite direction. Each time I saw him, he looked worse. His drinking had slowed a bit, but only because his health had taken a drastic turn for the worse. His years of drinking were catching up to him.

Before I knew it 1995 rolled around. With it came many life-changing events for me as well as my remaining sibling, Kerry. One warm day in June, I received a phone call from my mom telling me my father had been taken to the hospital. He had so many problems it was impossible for her to tell me what exactly was wrong. In a nutshell, his internal organs were like hamburger. If I were to offer a description, I would compare it to an automobile that had been neglected of maintenance for years. Virtually every part needed to be replaced or repaired.

Kerry was once again saddled with the unenviable job of escorting a dying family member to the hospital, except this time there wasn't an ambulance. Kerry was the ambulance. My father's discomfort had become so intolerable he summoned Kerry at once. He begged her to take him to the hospital. She suggested they call an ambulance, but he insisted there was no time for an ambulance, claiming the pain was unbearable. She reluctantly agreed and off they went to Dubuque. He was in agony. His body remained curled up in a fetal position the entire way. Kerry pleaded for him to hang on. The last thing she wanted was for him to die in her car.

When they arrived at the hospital it wasn't a moment too soon. The second my father crossed the threshold of the hospital doors he collapsed and fell into a deep coma. Shortly after Kerry had made it to the hospital, I received the call from my mother informing me of the news. When I heard it, I notified my work of the situation and they immediately granted me leave. I packed my things and left for Dubuque in a hurry.

During the drive up I thought of all the times my father had forced his wrath upon me and the rest of the family. It hardly seemed possible he was on the verge of death. I had always believed he was too mean to die. I wasn't convinced yet. I told myself I would only believe it when I saw it. I thought of my mother, I knew it wasn't going to be easy for her.

You would have thought by now that someone as battle tested with death as me would have certainly sorted out my feelings toward my father. If put in my shoes, the average Joe may have welcomed his passing, but instead, I found myself more confused than ever as to what, and how, I felt.

When I arrived at the hospital, Kerry and my mom were already there. Only the machines were keeping him alive now. He had a living will, so the decision to remove him from life support would rest squarely on my mom's shoulders. All eyes turned toward her, waiting to see what she would do. Looking at her, I could see the pain written all over her face. I couldn't escape the irony of how she now held his life in her hands after she had been held captive by him for so many years. Had she wanted him gone I don't think any of us would have objected. However it was a little more complicated than that. Neither Kerry nor I could have possibly comprehended what was going on inside of her. Clearly she still loved him. Torn by having to make such a difficult decision, she decided to wait it out a couple more days.

On June 12, 1995, my father was removed from life support. He was sixty-four years old. In an extreme state of sobriety, I told myself it was finally over. His death signaled more than just an end to his life. Once and for all, those of us who survived were finally released from him forever. It was officially over, but not emotionally.

I still wasn't quite sure what I felt for my father. I was engulfed by a flood of emotions. Among these were anger, pity, heartbreak, and most of all, regret. Regret because of how things could have been different. For a Christian, being able to forgive is essential to Christ's way of life. I knew all too well how often I had needed forgiveness in my own life. Why was it so difficult for me to forgive him now?

It's hard to pinpoint, but there was a definite part of my father that I did love. In between the binges and the hangovers and whenever he wasn't being a bastard, which I remind you didn't occur very often, we had made a connection as father and son. Although fleeting, there had been brief flashes of love that carried with them the promise of change and the possibility of a better life. Sadly, over time, those flashes flickered, until finally they were extinguished altogether.

My father lacked just about every parenting skill needed to properly raise a family. His inability to overcome the demon of alcoholism proved insurmountable for him. It consumed him in the end. I'm not sure if I'll ever come to grips with his life or death. I have conceded that within God's infinite plan, there are just some things that surpass human understanding.

My mother, sister, and I all cried when my father died. I knew my mom would cry, but up until the moment it happened, I was uncertain as to how either Kerry or I would react. I think we all cried for different reasons. Looking at his lifeless body, I was reminded that despite his faults, he was still my father. I wouldn't have had a life if it weren't for him. I knew I had to forgive him or I'd remain a slave to hatred forever. So slowly, over time, I did forgive him. I can honestly say I no longer despise my father for how he was and what he did to his family. Hate is such a strong emotion that leaves no room for redemption. I had no desire or right to pass judgment. His was a tormented soul. I concluded this was more than enough punishment.

It was agonizing to see my mom grieving again. She had already endured so much pain in her life. I could only wonder what was going through her mind. I'm sure she wept for many different reasons. The biggest of these had to have been the broken promises of an abusive marriage. I'm sure seeing him dead now made her relive the deaths of their children. This had to hang heavy in her heart. Despite it all, she still loved him. I guess if you've spent the greater share of your life with someone, it's a good thing to be able to say you loved them. Lacking words of encouragement, I comforted her with a big hug. By the look on her face, I could tell the hug was better than anything I could have ever said.

Up to this time I had often wondered why my mother chose to stay with my father rather than just divorce him. Certainly she should have done it; if not for herself, then at the very least for the sake of her children. Once, in a quiet moment, I asked my mom this very question. Her response was predictable. She told me my father repeatedly threatened to kill her if she ever left him. His use of fear had always been on an up-close-and-personal level. This was no exception. It was more than just another one of his scare tactics. He was playing for keeps. Besides, she had no intention of testing the waters of his threat. She knew he was crazy enough to follow through with it. Having experienced his psychosis firsthand, I of all people should have known this. After all, fear was his signature trademark. It made perfect sense. I was sorry I had ever asked.

Other than the day when my grandmother removed John from our home, I can only recall one instance when someone stood up to my father during one of his terrible tirades. That "someone" was my brother John. At the time, I was still in high school. John had just returned home for the first time since joining the army. Shortly before his arrival, my father had recently gone through one of his drunken rampages. It culminated with the beating of my mother, the effects of which left visible marks on her face and body. When John saw her battered body he stormed our house like a man on a mission. I was there the day all hell broke loose. My father was perched in his usual spot at the kitchen table reading his newspaper, just as he had when we were small children. Enraged with anger, John burst into the house, his body clearly surging from an adrenaline rush. He began threatening my father by saying, "If you ever lay a finger on my mother again, I will kill you!" In retaliation my father stood up out of his chair to face his son. With a defiant intensity he began shouting back at John, but before he could finish, John grabbed him by his arms and shoved him back sending him crashing through the kitchen wall. Inside, I was jumping up and down in a long-awaited victory dance. You would've thought the Cubs had just won the World Series! However, on the outside I was as calm as a cucumber, for I knew even the slightest hint of disloyalty would later spell retaliation for me. It was almost impossible to hold back the applause. For the first time ever, my father was on the receiving end of an uncontrollable rage. I know it's un-Christian, but I couldn't deny the gratification I felt when I witnessed him getting a dose of his own medicine.

Unfortunately, this incident only served to strengthen his resolve over us. I truly believe he was incapable of changing. Not even the deaths of his own children made him depart from his callous ways. With his death, the dark cloud that had hovered over us for so many years was finally lifted. We were prisoners then, but we were free now.

While his death signaled the end of one era, it also ushered in the beginning of another. A big part of each of us died with him that day, but from those ashes arose three new people. We were finally free of him. Almost instantaneously our lives changed for the better. Within a short time, Kerry's first marriage came to an abrupt end. Soon after, she found and married the man of her dreams. Later that same year, I ended my long-term failed relationship only to meet the woman of my dreams as well. Incredibly, the two of us had stumbled upon our soul mates by no effort of our own. The timing of this seemed to confirm the notion we could never experience true peace until we were fully released from him. Our newfound happiness brought tremendous comfort to my mother. It was our defining example of good coming from bad.

A New Beginning

My mom first met my future wife, Aimee, when Kerry got married for the second time. I brought her home for the wedding and to meet the family. I first met Aimee when she worked for my company as a seasonal employee. I was immediately drawn to her, but when the holidays ended, she left the company. Shortly after her departure, my failed relationship of eleven years came to a screeching halt. When it was over, I remember praying to God, asking him to bring me a true and lasting love. I was stunned when Aimee returned to my store after accepting a regular position with the company. I had never seen a more beautiful woman in my life. I was convinced God had sent her back to me. It wasn't long before we fell hopelessly in love with each other. God had answered my prayer by bringing me a soul mate.

It wasn't long after Kerry's wedding when my mother experienced a serious setback in her health. For a number of months she had been self-doctoring what was believed to have been a spider bite on one of her legs. The wound ate a huge hole in her calf muscle. In addition to improperly treating the wound, her history of poor circulation turned the ordeal into a life-threatening situation. She was rushed to the hospital with neither Kerry nor I even remotely aware of what was wrong. A circulatory doctor was called in. The prognosis was not good. The infection from the wound had gone untreated for so long that it appeared her leg would have to be amputated. I was furious when Kerry informed me of my mother's pitiful attempt at self-healing. I had to do my best to contain my frustration with her. I'm not sure which was worse, my anger or my worry.

I immediately made plans for an emergency visit to the hospital in Galena. By the time I arrived at the hospital my curiosity over the seriousness of her wound had nearly driven me insane. After giving her a lecture and a hug, I examined her wound. I found it to be as deep as it was wide. The area was dark maroon in color and larger than a silver dollar. It literally took the wind out of my sail to view it. I couldn't help but visualize her caring for this painful wound with nothing more than some gauze and a tube of insect bite ointment. I suppose after losing three children it's no wonder why my mother had such little faith in modern medicine.

I continued making numerous trips back and forth while the uncertainty of whether or not she would lose her leg hung in the balance. She was undergoing extensive daily treatments to heal her leg. After a couple months of this the doctors came forth with good news and bad news. The good news was they had saved her leg. The bad news was she would be restricted to a wheelchair and require indefinite daily care. Her only alternative was to sell her home and take up permanent residency at the Galena nursing home. Convincing her to do this would not be easy. It pained me to tell her, but there were really no other options. Reluctantly, she gave into reality. She slowly adjusted to her new life in the nursing home by doing what she had done for most of her life, making the best of a situation over which she had little control.

In November of 1996, I married Aimee in a small United Methodist Church no bigger than the one I had attended as a child. Kerry and her new husband, Chuck, had promised to make the trip to St. Louis to attend the wedding. When my mother learned of our upcoming nuptials, she promised me nothing would keep her from being there. However, there was still a great deal of speculation as to whether or not her doctors would allow her to come. I knew being cooped up in a car for six hours would pose a difficult challenge for her. I prayed to God hoping he could give her the strength to come. A few days before the wedding,

Kerry called me with the best wedding present I could have ever hoped for, my mother's presence.

Our wedding date was November 9. I waited all day for her arrival. I cringed each time I thought of her having to endure the six-hour drive to St. Louis. Aimee and I, along with Tyler and Mallory, arrived at the church about an hour before the ceremony. The wedding party had already assembled. I was pacing back and forth, although this wasn't from pre-marriage jitters. Marrying Aimee was the surest thing I had ever done in my life. I was nervous because Kerry, her family, and my mom had yet to show. My worrying came to an end when they arrived shortly before the ceremony began. I insisted on pushing her wheelchair up the long sloping handicap ramp that led to the church entrance. As we rolled up the ramp, a miraculous thing took place. Big, white, fluffy snowflakes began gently falling from above. Before entering the church, we paused for a moment to marvel at the first snow of the coming winter season. I was moved beyond words. My mother placed her hand on mine and said, "It looks like the good Lord himself is consummating your marriage." It was definitely a sign from heaven.

A little more than a year later, on the night our son Zachary was born, the biggest, whitest, fluffiest snowflakes I had ever seen in my life began falling straight down from above, once again appearing to be heaven sent. Even more incredible, just a few weeks later, our first Christmas together as a family was highlighted by yet another beautiful snow of similar magnificence. Now, I'm sure some people would write these occurrences off as coincidence, but as you already know, I stopped believing in coincidence a long time ago. For me, there was no mistaking these beautiful snowfalls, especially when they occurred at such significant moments in my life. These three events assured me God was as happy for us as we were for ourselves.

For my mother, there was one comfort that never failed to elevate her spirit, that being a visit from her newest grandchild. Zach's birth was unique in the sense that there had not been a new grandchild in the family for over ten years. It would be an understatement to say my mom loved having a baby back in the family. Aimee and I made numerous trips to the nursing home so she and Zach could spend time together. I loved watching her face light up each time Zach came for a visit. I have always treasured these moments.

Leaving the nursing home was never easy. I still felt the need to rescue her. The nursing home was almost as depressing of an environment as her life had been with my father. Unfortunately, there was little I could do to change it. I tried to make the best of it by visiting her as often as I could. On more than one occasion, if she was feeling up to it, Aimee and I would take her out of the nursing home for a drive. We usually took her shopping and then out for dinner. She truly loved these temporary escapes. They were good times.

When the spring of 1999 rolled around, I managed to get away from work for a weekend to take a trip up to see my mom. Although our visit was short, she looked better than the last time we had visited. She had become quite popular with many of her fellow residents. As a result of this, she was elected president of the residence board. Her duties consisted mostly of selecting and leading events for the residents. Her new title had given her a spark, making our visit even more enjoyable. Before leaving, I told her I had planned a week of vacation in June so we could spend some quality time together. She smiled and told me she would look forward to it with great anticipation. Sadly, before that time came, I received a call from the nursing home informing me that my mom had passed away in her sleep. My poor mother, who had suffered through so much, had quietly slipped into an eternal rest. I was overcome with grief, partly for her passing, but mainly for all of the years of suffering she had endured during her life. Once again I harbored those familiar regrets of not being able to make her life better. Aimee reminded me that she was better, for her two remaining children had found true love and she no longer worried for their happiness. To her, it was more than she could have ever hoped for.

I can honestly say I've always loved my mother with all of my heart. She was always there for us. She was the one constant in our otherwise unstable lives. She always put us first, often at the expense of depriving herself of life's simplest pleasures. She was truly the best. Her unconditional love for her children yielded countless demonstrations of self-sacrifice. My only wish was that she could have experienced a little more happiness. She definitely deserved a better life.

Whenever I think of my mom, my fondest memories of her are those with all of us kids just hanging out while my father was away immersing himself at the tavern. She had freely given each of us the two most precious commodities any human being has to offer, time and love. Time has become so valuable to me. She always told me to be conscious of my time, as well as the time of others. She often reminded me to be wise in how and with whom I spent it. She once said, "Time is a limited resource and is far more precious than any material thing." It took me a great deal of time to learn that lesson.

The Tree

Over the next couple of years I continued to return to Hanover each summer to visit my sister Kerry and her family. I also made regular pilgrimages to the cemeteries to pay my respects at the gravesites of my lost family members. I found myself strangely drawn to their final resting places. My grandparents and Eydie had been laid to rest in the New Cemetery while John, Sara, and my parents were in the Old Cemetery. The Old and New Cemeteries hadn't changed much since my youth. Whenever I visited their graves, I was hit by a flood of lawn-mowing memories. Those fond days now felt like a lifetime ago. The longer I stood there the harder it was for me to stay. Graveyards can be fickle places. I knew the stones that marked their graves were nothing more than a mere shadow of who they were. Despite this truth, the symbolism the stones cast weighed heavy on my heart.

During these visits home, I continued to search for old friends, especially the Wiffle Ball Elites. The local bars had pretty much become what the town hall used to be. After frequenting a few of the local establishments, it didn't take long for me to run across a couple of the old Elites who still lived in the Hanover area. However, Jim Cottral, an Elite who I really wanted to catch up with, remained elusive every time I returned home for a visit. I learned he was now living in nearby Freeport, Illinois. I was told he often came back on the weekends, but our timing seemed to be off as we kept missing each other each time I came back.

In 2003, our paths finally crossed at my twenty-fifth high school reunion. Jim confessed he almost decided not to come but changed his mind at the last minute. Jim held a legendary status as a second-generation "Wiffle Ball Elite," but he was more than just a comrade of the great old game. As kids, we spent countless hours fishing on the banks of the Apple River. We also got into our share of mischief now and then. It was a blast to finally see him and relive some of those fond memories from our childhood. I must admit I was more excited to see him than any of my classmates. Jim was just a fun-loving guy who never got wrapped up in the competition of life. He lived and let live. I admired him for that.

After the reunion, he invited Aimee and me over to his place. Through the years he had acquired some land and built a house five miles northwest of town. It's a beautiful place surrounded by gorgeous countryside. To fully appreciate its splendor, he invited us to come back next year and stay for a weekend. Since Aimee and I are avid hikers, this was a special treat for us. We couldn't wait to come back.

When Aimee and I returned in April of the following year, the place looked even more beautiful in the spring. His homestead was situated on the south side of a big ridge overlooking a valley of fields and timber. He had built a pond just a short distance before the southern most edge of his property line. The pond was a perfect finishing touch to an already majestic scene. I felt extremely fortunate to have finally met up with Jim again. Staying out at his place and partaking in his little slice of paradise was a huge added bonus.

One morning while hiking around his place, I happened to notice a large old cottonwood tree tucked away in the valley where his ranch sat. It suddenly dawned on me that Jim's property was situated in the general vicinity of where "the tree" from my childhood memories was believed to have been. South Blanding Road was less than a mile west of Jim's place. I had always been told the tree was located somewhere in the woods on the west side of this road. When I got back to the house, I had to ask him if he was familiar with the tree and its presumed location.

It turned out that Jim was more than just aware of the tree's existence. He had recently learned that "The Tree's" true location was actually on his side of South Blanding Road. Jim went on to say that Jack White, an old timer who had attended numerous gatherings at "The Tree," had recently stopped out to see his place. While chatting, Jack brought up the subject wondering if Jim had ever stumbled across the remains of the famous tree. Jim acknowledged he had heard of the tree but was unaware of its precise location. Soon after Jack had revealed to him the the tree's general location, he made a thorough search of the area in question but was unable to locate any remains.

After hearing this information, I asked Jim if it was okay for Aimee and me to do some searching for ourselves. Being the gracious host that he was, he encouraged us to do so but was unable to join us because he had to work the next day. He told us we could cross any fence we came to, for he was good friends with all of his neighbors. He simply said, "If anyone stops you, just tell them you're staying with Jim Cottral and everything will be fine."

By now, I was getting pretty excited. Aimee and I had already planned to do some hiking around Jim's property the next morning, but in my eyes we had now received a higher calling. That night I plotted a search area. Aimee didn't seem to mind me turning our leisurely hike into a big tree safari. She was well aware of my obsession with the tree.

We awoke the next day to sunny skies and cool temperatures. It was a perfect day for a hike. We ate some breakfast and took off in the direction of the timber that dominated the east side of South Blanding Road. After hiking through some of the nearby fields, we crossed a fence and a short distance later reached the edge of the timberline. After crossing another fence, we entered into the dense woods. Once inside the forest we found no visible trail to follow. Undeterred, we simply made our own path. Fortunately it was still early spring, which meant the forest undergrowth had yet to flourish.

As we meandered through the woods, I recognized some of the various hardwoods and softwoods that existed within this classic Midwestern stand of forest. Cherry, oak, elm, maple, and cottonwood were abundant. Their presence created a calming effect on me. We walked a short distance farther before discovering a big cottonwood tree that must have been at least fifteen feet around. Despite its towering size, it was still a far cry from the dimensions of the tree. Nevertheless, it was still a thing of beauty. On a positive note, we viewed this giant as a good omen. Its presence confirmed we were smack dab in the middle of an ideal environment in which large cottonwoods could thrive.

Aimee and I continued hiking through the woods, zigzagging our way across the rugged terrain. Our search yielded nothing. There was no sign of the tree. By the time we reached the next fence, we were straddling South Blanding Road. We had systematically covered the most viable stretch of land where the tree was reportedly to have existed. It was disappointing, but there were still a couple of other stands of timber to be investigated. Midday was fast approaching. With the sun high above our heads, we decided to eat our sack lunch before moving on to the next search area. I had a strong feeling if we didn't find the tree here, we probably weren't going to find it at all. Only my obsession with finding the tree kept me from confiding this foregone conclusion with Aimee. We discussed our options. The next best search area wasn't even close to the vicinity of where Jack White had reportedly said the tree was supposed to be. Part of me just wanted to give up. That feeling kept growing stronger by the minute. Aimee, sensing my disappointment, told me, "Well, at least it has been a good hike." We finished our lunch and began making our way back through the thicket.

While heading out of the forest, I spotted a fence running parallel to the tree line. Alongside of it was an open field that offered an easier route to the next search area. Traversing the fence was a wooden step bridge that offered us easy access across. We started hiking toward it in single file. I reached the step bridge first, and while making my way over, I looked back to check on Aimee. Off in the distance, I noticed what appeared to be a huge fallen tree lying in a dense thicket. It obviously wasn't the tree for it was clearly lacking in size. It was, however, fairly accessible, so I told Aimee I wanted to get a closer look.

Slowly we made our way back into the uninviting jungle. The closer we got to the log the more visible it became. It was certainly of good size all right, probably close to fifteen feet in width. When I got to within a few feet, a massive cluster of thicket stood between me and the log. Refusing to be denied access, I was left with no other choice but to circumnavigate around this conglomeration of entangled foliage. Aimee informed me if I intended to explore it any further I'd have to do it on my own. While searching for a way around the brush, I discovered a hidden corridor naturally formed by the encroaching canopy. It allowed easy passage through the otherwise dense thicket. Ducking my head and crouching, I made my way through Mother Nature's tunnel. Once through, a clearing opened up on the other side. I stood back up, and, to my bewilderment, I discovered a second dead tree of equal size! The overgrowth had completely hidden it from our view. This was getting very interesting.

A closer inspection began to unravel the mystery. My initial assessment had been wrong. I wasn't looking at two different trees; I was actually looking at one. In the midst of these two sleeping giants was the remnant of a taproot. Splintered, but still intact, it jutted up over four feet out of the ground! When the two giants collapsed on opposite sides of each other, the taproot must have snapped, leaving it in this prominent position.

Further examination revealed a couple of extraordinary clues. A piece of bark that had to have been ten feet in length and two feet in width was resting between the two giants. I dislodged it from a layer of flora that had entwined itself around the bark. The bark was over two inches thick! After closely examining this artifact, I gained a position where I could take in the full scene. I easily determined that this tree was definitely a classic V-shaped cottonwood, exactly like the one I had seen in my father's photograph as a kid so many years ago.

Some of the giant cottonwood trees characteristically grow in a drooping V shape. Two massive spires start out as one until eventually splitting off in opposite directions. I quickly made some rough estimates of each log to determine if its overall size was consistent with that of the tree. It didn't take long to deduce that the combined width of the two spires measured nearly twenty-five feet in circumference, almost the exact same size as the tree!

By now, Aimee hadn't heard a peep out of me in quite a while. She must have wondered what on earth I was doing. When I heard her call out my name, I excitedly called back to her with instructions on how to find the hidden corridor so she could join me. Not wanting to take my eyes off the prize, I finally came to my senses by helping her get to the vantage point I had been enjoying. Like a little kid in a candy store, I started talking to myself, "Surely this is the colossal tree I so vividly recall from my childhood." But how was I to know for sure if this really was the tree?"

Moments later, indisputable proof came forth in the form of a familiar voice from the present, not the past. Yes, it was none other than my darling wife, Aimee. She had uncovered the irrefutable proof that had been buried for years underneath one of the giant columns. I looked up at her and there, resting in her hand, was a slightly crushed, slightly rusted, but unmistakable Hamm's beer can. Seeing the artifact with its bright blue emblems cascading up and down the sides of the can warmed my heart; I'm sure in the same way as it had done to my father every time he cracked one open. A shiver ran up and down my spine. Lo and behold, I had found the tree.

The circle was finally complete. What was once lost, had now been found. For me, it was a discovery of an unimaginable proportion. Years of wonder instantly gave way as I stood in the presence of this once magnificent living thing. I thought, *All things are possible with God.* Not only did finding the tree fulfill my childhood curiosity, it symbolically reaffirmed my belief that not everything is lost with death.

A short distance from the sight, we found another classic V-shaped cottonwood standing tall and proud. It was an impressive tree in its own right, nearly twenty feet around. Next to this beauty we discovered a huge pile of Hamm's beer cans. I picked up one of the sacred relics and took it back to Jim's house where I cleaned it up and reverently placed it on top of his refrigerator. It still resides there today. Call it superstition, but I had no intention of letting that can leave the area. After all, it had been resting there for so long. Disturbing it any further would have been a sacrilege, like desecrating a shrine or trespassing on an ancient Indian burial ground. I figured, *As long as it remains near the sight, no curse will be provoked.*

When Jim heard the news, he couldn't believe we had found the tree. In fact, he refused to believe it until he saw it for himself. I couldn't help but think of Doubting Thomas from the New Testament. The next day we hiked down to the site together. Once he saw the remains for himself, he was satisfied that it was indeed the tree.

Rediscovering the tree was something I could have only dreamed. The privilege of being the first person to stand in its presence in such a long time was truly the greatest honor I could have ever hoped for. It was like reuniting with an old friend who had vanished without a trace many years ago. I couldn't help but think of the photograph of my father along with his buddies having such a good time. For the first time in my life, I felt like I stood in a complete and no longer broken circle with him.

Since its discovery, I have returned to visit the tree every year. I have photographed it from just about every angle imaginable. Regardless of its demise, its sheer size still impresses today despite some twenty years of decay. People say you should never live in the past, but after locating the tree I found it hard not to. For some, our past shapes our future by reminding us of where we came from and where we're headed. Everything happens for a reason. There is no coincidence. Don't hang on too tightly to the past, but don't entirely let go either. Remember, history can repeat itself unless we learn from it.

Good Coming from Bad

I'm sure everyone at one time or another has heard the phrase "white as snow." In the Bible, this phrase is mentioned several times. In the New Testament, it is mentioned twice, once in Matthew to describe the angel of the Lord who pushed aside the stone to open the path for the risen Lord. The second time it appears in Mark, when he describes the transfiguration of Elijah, Moses, and

Jesus. These are two of the most powerful moments in Scripture if not *the* most powerful.

Someone once said, "People are just like snowflakes, each one uniquely designed with no two being exactly the same." You know how much snowflakes have come to play a big part in my life. Through my experience even the most insignificant relationships take on serious meaning. Every breath we take should be viewed as an invaluable gift given to us from our Creator. Our time here is so short, literally a blink of the eye in comparison to time itself. Taking people for granted is no longer an option for me. Making the most out of seemingly dull moments has become my mantra in life.

The first half of my life was filled with pain and misery. Fortunately, the Lord taught me how good can come from bad. He also taught me there's a big difference between having nothing and being nothing. This ultimately brought renewal to my broken spirit and hence made me rethink my value system and restructure my priorities to be more in tune with the teachings of Jesus Christ. It has now become my duty to spread the good news by proclaiming the universal bond we are all capable of receiving.

Not long ago I became engaged in a heated conversation with a non-believer over the age-old question, "Is God real?" Our discussion came to a head when he asked me the question, "If God is alive, then why doesn't he just show himself?" Let's ponder that question for a moment. What would really happen if God suddenly appeared before us? One day he will. But for now, take comfort in knowing that God is the giver of life, not the creator of robots. If he were to appear, everything would be answered and made easy for us. What could we possibly gain from that? He intended for us to have choices. He wants us to be challenged. He wants us to experience growth on our own. He wants us to learn what faith is. He is preparing us for something bigger and better. Think of our lives here on earth as a training ground, and even though he chose us, he still very much wants us to choose him. What makes this such a struggle is our sin. But it is that same sin that opens our eyes and hearts to him. For when we fall prey to sin, we often gain a deeper understanding of such qualities as humility, accountability, atonement, and forgiveness. It is through our suffering that we become molded into who we are. I'm living proof of that. It's kind of like good coming from bad.

However, our sin is also what makes us imperfect. That is why we remain separated from him. It is also true that on our own, sin is insurmountable. That is why God sent his only Son, Jesus Christ, into the world so our sins could be forgiven and we could have a way to the Father. Our faith in Christ is the only connection we have to God. Confess him as Lord and Savior of your life and I promise you'll find everything you were ever looking for. Is it really that difficult to see? If you really want to see the Lord, then look no further than to a true believer. It is there you will find him, for he can change lives. In my entire life experience I can only think of three sure things in this world, my wife, my family, and Jesus Christ. Oh yeah, the non-believer I was speaking these very words to has since begun reading the words of Christ to find out for himself what Jesus is all about. I challenge you to do the same, for through the Word you will find the answer.

One thing I never mentioned before was that shortly after the deaths of my loved ones, I felt I *had* to believe in the afterlife, for it was the only means I had of seeing them again. But then, once I had reaccepted Christ back into my life, I learned it was no longer a question of *if* I would see them, but rather *when* I would see them. If you've not found the Lord, then I hope, like in my case, he finds you. Trust me on this one. He is truly all we have. Stop wasting your time on earthly treasures and seek eternal treasures instead. Make no mistake about it; our time in this world has been measured. Don't waste a single breath. Make each of your minutes count by filling them with random acts of kindness to all who cross your path. Friendships and loved ones come and go in the wink of an eye. If you're a parent, thank God for your child and be sure to kiss them and tell them you love them every day. If you're not a parent, then thank God for your life, for all good things come from him. Most importantly, stay near to the Lord, and in return, he will always stay near you. Lastly, remember most of all, there *is* life after death.

Poems by Sarah Winter

These following two poems were written by my grandmother nearly forty years ago. My wife, Aimee, stumbled across them shortly after I had finished the book. They share an uncanny similarity with many of the stories in the book, almost as if they were written for that sole purpose.

Nostalgia

I've been walking down the road
that leads to my old home,
and wandering in the byways
as I child I used to roam.
And my heart was full of tears
as I ponder in the years…
yearning for the loved ones
that are gone.
There's the cottage on the hill,
in the sunshine warm and still,
and an old shack where we children
played so long,
But the one who made it home,
no longer bids me come.
There's a vacant place
no one can ever fill.
So I'm wandering down the road
that leads from my old home.
I'm not lingering in the byways
I no longer care to roam.
For my heart is full of tears
as I recall the long lost years
and the many loved ones that
are gone.

By Sarah Winter–1976

I Like It Here

I like it here
on the banks of the Apple,
where the warm summer breeze
in the cottonwood trees
sets the river a-dapple
I like it here
in the calm, quiet valley,
where each one you meet
has a bright smile to greet,
and time to visit or dally.
I like it here
where church steeples call us
to worship on Sunday,
it's wash day on Monday;
and long quiet evenings to lull us.
I like it here
where you hear children's laughter,
music is birdsong
all the day long
you hear the rivers soft chatter
I like it here
for here I found my dream,
let me sleep here forever
near the banks of the river,
let the voice of the water be my requiem.

By Sarah Winter–1970

Winter's Past

When I was a child, my grandfather on the Winter side often spoke of a couple of dynamic ancestors who made lasting impressions on him. The first of which was Henry Winter, who would have been my grandfather's grandfather and my great great grandfather. Henry was a member of the 45th Illinois Regiment during the Civil War. He originally enlisted as a bugler but later served as a drummer boy. Several intriguing stories surround his life. The first of which is how he came to the aid of a soldier who had been severely wounded during the battle of Vicksburg. The soldier's name was Wilbur Crummer. Henry discovered Wilbur while he lay wounded on the battlefield. Henry brought him to the surgeon's tent, but the surgeons refused to operate on him because they believed his wounds were not recoverable. Despite their assessment, Henry refused to leave the side of his fallen comrade.

Henry, with the aid of a sergeant, who also took up Wilbur's plight, diligently cared for him day and night until he slowly recovered from his wounds. Years later, Henry received several letters from Wilbur Crummer. In them, he spoke volumes of Henry's character and repeatedly thanked him for saving his life.

Henry himself did not leave the war unscathed. In February of 1862, at the battle of Fort Donelson, Henry was struck in the head by a Confederate mini ball. A short time later, his family received his death certificate. However, Henry was still alive, and, just like Wilbur, he had been left for dead on the battlefield. There's also a chilling account of how Henry's body laid motionless amongst the many corpses strewn across the battlefield. When the gravediggers were burying the dead, one of their shovels accidentally struck Henry's leg. To their horror Henry let out a moan. Mortified, they carried him to the surgeon's tent, where he successfully had the slug removed from his head. He spent weeks recuperating before returning to active duty. However, several metal shards remained in his head. These shards brought on terrible headaches whenever he was exposed to bright sunshine. In the years that followed he was forced to wear a hat to protect him from the now punishing rays of the sun.

I have often wondered what it must have been like when his family was notified of his death in combat, only later to find out that he was still alive. I'm sure there was both joy and anger.

In May of 1863, he was captured at the Battle of Champion Hills but was paroled three months later and once again returned to active duty. Henry would participate in ten different battles during the Civil War before being honorably discharged in September of 1864.

Perhaps the most famous story of Henry centered on his Civil War drum. After the war, Henry kept his drum. It turned out that the drum he owned was quite rare. What made the drum special was a unique engraving of an American bald eagle on one of its sides, this distinguished it from many of the other drums used by the Union forces during the war.

The drum was handed down to the firstborn son in the family line until it ended up in the hands of my grandfather. My grandfather kept the drum for several decades until a squabble broke out between him and one of his brothers. His brother felt the drum should be sold and the funds dispersed proportionately among the surviving siblings. My grandfather refused to give in to these selfish desires and put a quick end to any possibility of this when he promptly donated the drum to the Galena Historical Society. Shortly after, it was put on display at the Galena museum. Needless to say, his brother was deeply angered by this decision, but he had little recourse once it became the property of the State of Illinois.

Galena, a picturesque town lined with architecture dating back to the mid-nineteenth century, is located just twenty minutes north of Hanover. Galena is the name given for the purest form of lead. Lead production in the Galena area reached its height just prior to the Civil War. Galena's lead resources made it a boomtown during the Civil War. Prior to the outbreak of the war, Galena was bigger than Chicago and boasted a prolific riverboat industry. It was also the home of the most famous Civil War general ever, Ulysses S. Grant. After the war, Grant took up residency in St. Louis, the lead and riverboat industry declined, and with it went Galena's prosperity. Today, Galena is experiencing a renaissance as many of the old buildings have been restored and converted into restaurants and shops. On a recent visit to the Galena museum, one of the staff informed me the Smithsonian Institute has been trying to get their hands on the drum for quite some time. So far, the Galena Historical Society has refused to part with the drum.

It continues to reside there with the rest of the museum's artifacts that date back to the Civil War and before.

Another famous character in Winter lore is a fellow by the name of William Johnson, who was better known as "Bushy" Bill. Bushy was Henry Winter's father-in-law, and, according to my grandfather, he could run like a fish and swim like a deer. Or was it the other way around? My grandfather often reminisced about him with a twinkle in his eye. He told me many stories of Bushy that predated the Blackhawk War. However, the most intriguing stories are those surrounding the Blackhawk War and his encounters with the great Indian chief, Blackhawk.

Chief Blackhawk was a brilliant tactician who commanded the last tribes to surrender their lands east of the Mississippi. Blackhawk's resistance delayed the settlement of the white man in Jo Daviess County and the surrounding area until superior numbers eventually forced him and his warriors to give up the fight.

The United States Army was befuddled at how a savage Indian chief with no military training could "out-general" some of the finest military minds of the day. It was this sort of arrogance that gave the ingenious Blackhawk the early upper hand in the conflict. What they didn't understand was that Blackhawk was no savage. He was an original American who courageously fought for his freedom, much in the same way as the patriots of our own American Revolution had done.

Fort Elizabeth, located smack dab in the middle of the territory that Chief Blackhawk and his warriors were fighting for, was a haven for settlers who sought protection from Blackhawk. The first engagement Bushy had with Blackhawk and his warriors occurred when Bushy was only eighteen years old. While most of the men who were stationed at the fort were out hunting for food, Blackhawk and his band staged a determined attack on the fort but were repeatedly repelled by Bushy and a few other men in their attempt to overtake the works. Only one man died in the attack. It happened to be a close friend of Bushy's who fell next to him as they fought side-by-side to defend their fort.

As a trailblazer and frontiersman, Bushy encountered the clever Indian chief on more than one occasion. According to my grandfather, he was captured and then somehow managed to escape the clutches of Blackhawk. In doing so, he further added to his reputation as a renowned woodsman forever gaining the respect of his fellow pioneers. I can't honestly say how much of Bushy's legend is true or not, but I do know that my grandfather was never the type to "drum up stories" for cheap entertainment. He believed the stories were true, and so do I.